The Bumper Student Cookbook

Good Housekeeping

The Bumper Student Cookbook

250 tried, trusted, tested recipes ★ delicious results

Compiled by Barbara Dixon

COLLINS & BROWN

First published in the United Kingdom in 2011 by
Collins & Brown
10 Southcombe Street
London
W14 0RA

An imprint of Anova Books Company Ltd

The Good Housekeeping website is
www.allboutyou.com/goodhousekeeping

10 9 8 7 6 5 4 3 2 1

ISBN 978-1-84340-608-2

A catalogue record for this book is available from the British Library.

Repro by Dot Gradations Ltd, UK
Printed and bound by Times Offset, Malaysia

This book can be ordered direct from the publisher at
www.anovabooks.com

Recipes in this book are taken from the Good Housekeeping recipe
library and may have been reproduced in previous publications.

PICTURE CREDITS
Neil Barclay (pages 82, 91, 100, 112, 167, 258, 260, 273, 275,
279 and 281); Martin Brigdale (pages 128, 129, 130, 131, 132,
134, 135, 136, 169, 170, 171, 176 and 200); Jean Cazals (page
103); Nicki Dowey (pages 39, 42, 44, 74, 75, 77, 78, 79, 81, 83,
84, 85, 88, 89, 92, 95, 96, 99, 102, 104, 105, 113, 114, 115,
116, 117, 118, 119, 120, 121, 122, 124, 125, 133, 140, 141,
143, 144, 145, 146, 147, 148, 149, 150, 151, 158, 159, 160,
161, 163, 164, 165, 166, 172, 173, 179, 180, 181, 182, 183,
188, 190, 192, 193, 194, 195, 201, 202, 203, 204, 206, 208,
209, 210, 211, 212, 213, 216, 217, 218, 219, 220, 222, 223,
224, 226, 232, 234, 235, 238, 239, 243, 245, 246, 247, 251,
252, 253, 254, 255, 256, 262, 263, 264, 269, 276, 278 and
282); Daniel Jones (page 184); Jonathan Lovekin (page 111);
Lis Parsons (pages 90, 177 and 198); Craig Robertson (pages 93,
94, 97, 98, 107, 110, 123, 137, 162, 185, 189, 191, 199, 205,
207, 221, 225, 227, 231, 244, 259, 268, 270, 271, 272, 274,
280 and 283); Lucinda Symons (pages 36, 37, 48, 58, 70, 71, 76,
80, 101, 142, 154, 156, 168, 230, 240, 257, 261 and 265);
Elizabeth Zeschin (page 241)
Stylists: Penny Markham, Wei Tang, Helen Trent, Fanny Ward and
Mari Mererid Williams
Home Economists: Anna Burges-Lumsden, Joanna Farrow, Emma Jane
Frost, Teresa Goldfinch, Alice Hart, Lucy McKelvie, Kim Morphew,
Katie Rogers, Bridget Sargeson, Stella Sargeson, Sarah Tildesley,
Jennifer White and Mari Mererid Williams

NOTES

Both metric and imperial measures are given for the
recipes. Follow either set of measures, not a mixture of
both, as they are not interchangeable.

All spoon measures are level.
1 tsp = 5ml spoon; 1 tbsp = 15ml spoon.

Ovens and grills must be preheated to the specified
temperature.

Medium eggs should be used except where otherwise
specified.

DIETARY GUIDELINES

Note that certain recipes contain raw or lightly
cooked eggs. The young, elderly, pregnant women
and anyone with immune-deficiency disease should
avoid these because of the slight risk of salmonella.

Note that some recipes contain alcohol. Check the
ingredients list before serving to children.

Contents

Foreword

I, rather predictably, grow nostalgic when thinking about the years spent at university. I've often thought about what exactly brings on this nostalgia without coming to a concise conclusion. It was my sister, with a similar sense of university-longing, who said, "Life as a student is straightforward". Spot on. Despite the complicated pursuit for academic excellence (naturally), you're mostly studying something you have chosen and enjoy. You have your pick of extra activities, from tiddlywinks to rugby, and you're surrounded by like-minded people. If you ever feel lonely, you simply have to saunter to the student bar or common room and no doubt you'll bump into a friendly face before you get there.

Once you've completed your course, the hours spent studying are often forgotten, but the rosy-tinted memories of fun, sporting trials, achievements, dinners (dare I say drinking!) and general geniality are fondly remembered.

Cooking in university digs can seem tough. With all the shared equipment and fridge-thievery that goes on, not to mention the disarray of dirty dishes and limited space; the odds seem to be stacked against you. But please don't be put off! Believe me, with a basic understanding of food and one bumper tried-and-tested cookbook, some of your happiest hours will be spent in the student kitchen. Mine were.

Student cooking is about simplicity, variation, ingredient substituting and impressing friends on a shoe-string. By cooking for yourself you can also save money, eat better and feed hungry friends. This student cookbook has it all, from hundreds of carefully chosen recipes (that are all guaranteed to work whatever your cooking ability) to helpful kitchen advice.

I wish I had this book when I set forth to student days, but seeing it come to fruition makes me equally proud. It's the only student cookbook you'll need.

I hope you enjoy this book and your college days – lucky you!

Meike.

Meike Beck
Cookery Editor

S ome student houses or flats come with a few pieces of cooking equipment – and perhaps a microwave – but most don't. Although it's easiest to cook with a variety of good utensils, it's amazing what you can get by without, but there are some essentials that you will certainly have to provide. There's no need to spend lots – cheaper shops have good selections that are fine for your student days. If you can invest in a good cook's knife, however, you will find it's worth the money. Have a look through the Essentials list and see how many things are already in your kitchen and then stock up with the others. Other useful items are also included for the keen cooks.

Stuff for the Kitchen

ESSENTIALS

PANS

☐ Three saucepans with lids: small, medium and large

☐ Large frying pan

MEASURING

☐ A 600ml (1 pint) measuring jug

☐ Measuring spoon

CUTTING, CHOPPING AND PEELING

☐ Three cook's knives: one large, one medium and a small serrated knife

☐ Bread knife

☐ Vegetable peeler

Baking without scales

As long as you have a tablespoon, you can measure out your baking ingredients without scales:

1 well-heaped tablespoon flour = 25g (1oz)

1 rounded tablespoon sugar = 25g (1oz)

Divide a block of butter in half to estimate 125g (4oz), in half again for 50g (2oz), and again for 25g (1oz)

- [ ] Kitchen scissors
- [ ] Two chopping boards: one for vegetables or cooked food and one for raw meat, fish or poultry

DRAINING, STIRRING AND TRANSFERRING

- [ ] A large sieve
- [ ] A large plastic spoon
- [ ] Wooden spoons

BOWLS

- [ ] Two different sized bowls

OVEN-COOKING

- [ ] A roasting tin
- [ ] Ovenproof cooking dish
- [ ] Flameproof casserole

HANDY UTENSILS AND OTHER ITEMS

- [ ] Can opener
- [ ] Corkscrew
- [ ] Kettle
- [ ] Tea towels
- [ ] Toaster

USEFUL TO HAVE

- [ ] A kitchen scale

BAKING

- [ ] A large mixing bowl
- [ ] 20.5cm (8in) springform cake tin
- [ ] Wire rack
- [ ] Baking parchment

STIRRING AND TRANSFERRING

- [ ] A whisk
- [ ] Rubber spatula (particularly if you like to bake)
- [ ] Tongs (handy for turning grilled foods and for serving spaghetti)

OVEN-COOKING

- [ ] A baking tray

HANDY UTENSILS AND OTHER ITEMS

- [ ] A grater
- [ ] Potato masher
- [ ] Rolling pin

ELECTRICAL EQUIPMENT

- [ ] Stick blender

If you've got a good basic storecupboard, fridge and freezer you won't be nipping out to the shops every day, but first you need to decide which kinds of foods you like to eat, as this will obviously affect your choices. Look through the lists below to see what you would realistically use in a week, then look through the recipes to see which other ingredients you need to add. Don't get carried away, though. It's easy to stock up on things that never get eaten, especially the perishables. (See page 22 for more about planning your week's shopping.)

Stocking Up

STORECUPBOARD BASICS

- [ ] Bread
- [ ] Cans of tomatoes, tuna
- [ ] Curry paste
- [ ] Dried mixed herbs
- [ ] Dried red lentils
- [ ] Mayonnaise
- [ ] Oils (olive, sunflower)
- [ ] Pasta and noodles
- [ ] Peanut butter
- [ ] Pulses (canned): red kidney beans, chickpeas, Puy lentils
- [ ] Basmati rice
- [ ] Salt and pepper
- [ ] Sauces (Worcestershire, soy, Tabasco, sweet chilli)
- [ ] Spices (curry powder, paprika, turmeric)
- [ ] Stock cubes (chicken, beef, vegetable, or vegetable bouillon)

- ☐ Sugar (caster)
- ☐ Tea and coffee
- ☐ Tomato ketchup and purée
- ☐ Vinegar (white or red wine)

EXTRAS

- ☐ Chutneys and pickles
- ☐ Cocoa powder
- ☐ Dried fruit (apricots, sultanas, raisins)
- ☐ Dried herbs (oregano, rosemary, thyme, sage, bay leaves)
- ☐ Flour (self-raising, plain)
- ☐ Jam, marmalade and honey
- ☐ Mustard (Dijon, English or wholegrain)
- ☐ Pesto
- ☐ Spices (cayenne, cinnamon, nutmeg)
- ☐ Tortilla wraps

FRIDGE

- ☐ Bacon
- ☐ Butter
- ☐ Cheese
- ☐ Eggs
- ☐ Yogurt
- ☐ Milk or soya milk

FREEZER

- ☐ Chicken breasts (frozen singly)
- ☐ Cooked prawns/mixed seafood
- ☐ Peas
- ☐ Sweetcorn

VEGETABLE RACK AND FRUIT BOWL

- ☐ Garlic
- ☐ Onions
- ☐ Potatoes
- ☐ Tomatoes
- ☐ Apples
- ☐ Bananas
- ☐ Lemon
- ☐ Oranges

You can eat well without spending a lot of money on food or fuel bills. Sometimes it takes a bit of planning ahead though. At other times it's just about saving any leftovers that you couldn't eat and heating them up for another day. Some of the tastiest suppers are simple, straightforward and cheap; Cottage Pie (see page 222) is one example, and many are quick to prepare – essential for the busy, and usually starving, student.

Living on a Budget

SIX WAYS TO SAVE MONEY

1   **Get organised** Make your list while you're actually in the house, and not on the road to the shops. Check what basics and staples you need for your storecupboard, fridge and freezer (see pages 10–11).

2   **Plan ahead** Think about what you fancy eating during the week and add that to your shopping list. It's cheaper to cook for two than one in the long run, so make double the amount for some meals, then cool and freeze half. Pasta sauces, such as Meat Sauce (see page 156), curries, casseroles and bakes can all be doubled up and frozen in this way.

3   **Share** shopping bills with friends.

4   **Shop sensibly** Stick to your shopping list and look for special offers.

5   **Use up your leftovers** Heat up that small portion of pasta sauce leftover from dinner the previous day to make a quick lunch.

6   **Check out** the market or supermarket at the end of the day and buy some marked-down foods, but only if you need them.

STRETCHING MEALS

Meat, poultry and fish can be expensive, but you can save pounds on your food budget and still eat filling, nutritious dishes.

You don't need to buy a giant piece of meat to serve one person. As a rough guide, a chicken breast weighing about 150g (5oz) will serve one; or buy double the weight and use for two meals.

Buy cheaper cuts of meat, such as chicken thighs and sausages. Casseroles and stews usually include plenty of vegetables, so you can just serve with bread if you like. Cook these dishes in bulk to save on fuel and then store in the fridge for up to three days or put in the freezer. Try Braised Meat (page 44) or Easy Chicken and Vegetable Hotpot (page 199).

Add canned beans and pulses to bulk out stews and casseroles, whether made with meat or without. Drain and rinse them first.

Remember that frozen food can be cheaper than fresh, so if you can store it buy it.

Leftover delights

There are plenty of recipes in this book that can be made with typical fridge leftovers:

LEFTOVER	RECIPE
Apples past their best	Express Apple Tart (page 281)
Bacon rashers	Bacon and Egg Salad (page 124), Quick and Easy Carbonara (page 157)
Cooked pasta	Quick Winter Minestrone (page 251), Fast Macaroni Cheese (page 166), Pasta with Pesto and Beans (page 165)
Cooked potatoes	Herring and Potato Salad (page 115)
Custard	Cheat's Chocolate Pots (page 275)
Mixed vegetables	Cheese and Vegetable Bake (page 258), Veggie Curry (page 265)
Pancake batter	Cinnamon Pancakes (page 278)
Pears past their best	Pear and Blackberry Crumble (page 280)
Salad	Bacon and Egg Salad (page 124), Easy Tuna Salad (page 116)
Savoy/white cabbage	Quick Winter Minestrone (page 251), Easy Chicken and Vegetable Hotpot (page 199)
Tomato sauce	Simple Meat Sauce (page 156)

FREEZING LEFTOVERS

If you have a freezer, you can freeze small portions of leftovers if you can't decide what to do with them right now – but don't forget them. It's a good idea to label them with your name, what the food is and a date.

One or two chillies Halve and deseed them, then freeze. They are easy to chop from frozen.

Fresh root ginger Peel then freeze. You can grate the ginger from frozen.

If you don't have a freezer

Most student houses have a fridge-freezer these days, but if your fridge only has an ice box, you won't realistically be able to store much of your own food there, as you will have to share the limited space with your housemates.

Talk to your housemates about how to use the space fairly and effectively.

Date stamps on food

Foods are stamped with a 'sell-by' or 'display until' date. This date is a guide to shop staff and it is not illegal to sell the item past that date; however, the food must also show a 'use-by' or 'best-before' date. Use-by dates are given on foods that go off quickly (such as milk, soft cheese, poultry, meat and ready-prepared meals). Do not eat foods after this date, as they may not be safe.

'Best-before' dates are added to foods that last longer (such as frozen, dried or canned foods). After this, you are encouraged to throw the food out and start again; however, with the odd exception, and using your judgement, you can simply check if it's OK to use by smell, look and feel. Follow your instincts: if it smells bad, looks off or has mould growing on it, bin it.

How to freeze

Never put hot or warm food in the freezer, always cool the food thoroughly then chill in the fridge first.

Freeze liquids, stews or soups in a container, or in a bag inside a container. Leave a space of 2.5cm (1in) at the top to allow the food to expand as it freezes. Cover tightly, label and freeze. Once frozen, remove the container and store in the bag.

To freeze meat, poultry and fish, put individual portions of the food in a freezer bag, keeping it flat. Squeeze all the air out so that the bag fits snugly around the food; this avoids 'freezer burn'. Tie or seal the bag securely, label and freeze.

Takeaways can be pretty tasty, and there are definitely times when cooking really does seem too much like a chore, but when you're trying to keep costs down (and perhaps aiming to eat healthily as well) it's a good idea to have a think and see what you can make that's just as appealing. There are lots of recipes in this book that are quick and simple to prepare, so they're light on labour as well as costing you less.

Cheaper Than a Takeaway

LUNCHES ON THE GO

Although there's lots of choice for lunch on the high street, the costs can add up. If you make your own lunches you'll save money, and they can taste much better too. Otherwise, use up leftovers in salads, wraps and sandwiches.

SOUP

You can't beat a homemade soup for a nutritious and warming meal. What's more, they are cheap to make and perfect for using up leftover vegetables. Try Quick Winter Minestrone (page 251).

PIZZA

Rather than buying a takeaway pizza, buy the bases and make your own. Spread over some tomato purée or Quick Tomato Sauce (page 154), then top with whatever you have in the fridge:

- Throw-it-all-together Naan Pizza (page 102)
- Tuna Melt Pizza (page 105)
- Garlic Cheese Pizza (page 104)

FRIDAY NIGHT TAKEAWAY

Many of us like a takeaway to finish up a long and tiring week, but they are expensive. Make your own takeaway alternative and it will save you money and taste fantastic. It won't take long to cook either; in fact, by the time you've ordered a meal from the local shop and picked it up or had it delivered, you could have whipped up one of these recipes yourself:

- Chicken Stir-fry with Noodles (page 137)
- Spiced Tikka Kebabs (page 150)
- Fish and Chips (page 226)

DESSERTS

An occasional sweet treat is one of life's pleasures, and homemade desserts can be quick to make. When you're feeling in the mood, try these:

- Strawberry and Chocolate Muffins (page 270)
- Quick Lemon Mousse (page 274)
- Quick Chocolate Slices (page 279)
- Pear and Blackberry Crumble (page 280)

It's the easiest thing to make delicious home-cooked food that is healthy – even when you're cooking on a budget. In fact, some of the healthiest foods are really cheap – take pulses, for example. A can of chickpeas costs pence, yet it can be whizzed up to make a hummus or added to a tomato and vegetable sauce or curry and served with pasta or rice for one of the healthiest meals you could find. Canned fish and cheaper cuts of chicken, such as thighs, make tasty, nourishing meals. Ready-made food, however, generally costs more to buy than fresh ingredients and usually has more salt, sugar and fat than you would add to your homemade version.

Eating Healthily

WHAT MAKES A HEALTHY MEAL?

- As a rough guide, fill about half your plate with plenty of vegetables as a good way of getting your 'five a day'. Always choose a variety, to get a wide range of nutrients. An easy way is to have a leafy green, plus something red or yellow at the least. Your protein portion will then take about a quarter of the plate and your rice or potatoes the other quarter. If you have a pasta dish you might like to eat it with a side salad.
- Always have a small amount of protein: meat, fish, eggs, beans, tofu, Quorn, seeds or nuts. Even if you're not a vegetarian, have some vegetarian meals in a week. They are cheap and tasty as well as nutritious.
- Eggs, oily fish, unsalted nuts and seeds contain 'essential' fats that your body needs for good health, so eat these regularly every week.
- Dairy foods can make simple and tasty meals. A cheese sauce goes well with vegetables or pasta, or yogurt takes the heat out of a curry. Be careful of adding cheese to too many meals, though, as you can have too much saturated fat this way. Saturated fat is found in dairy foods and meat and has been linked to ill health and obesity, so it's wise to keep portions of cheese small and have just a light spreading of butter. Go for leaner cuts of meat or trim off the fat, if possible.
- Accompany each meal with filling bread, rice, potatoes, pasta or other starchy foods – choose wholegrain varieties whenever you can.

WHAT ABOUT LABELLING?

Although there is now a traffic-light scheme developed by the Food Standards Agency to help us know how healthy a food is, the fact remains that if you want to eat well you need to cook as many meals as you can from scratch.

Here are the guidelines for bought foods: a red, amber or green colour coding is given for high, medium or low quantities of calories, sugar, fat, saturated fat and salt. Obviously, green is the one you want to aim for. Guideline Daily Amounts (GDAs) are also listed on foods, and these give an indication of how many calories, fat, salt, sugar and fibre a food contains and what percentage of the total recommended daily intake each of them constitutes (based on 2,000 calories, which is the average requirement for an adult woman).

Use labelling as a guide, if you like, but as a rule of thumb if you stick to buying the food in its most basic state (cans of tomatoes or fish, tubes of tomato purée, fresh or frozen vegetables, fresh meat and poultry, and so on) you'll have more control over what you eat.

Hidden salt

Salt is not good for us in anything but the tiniest quantities, but did you know that three-quarters of all the salt we eat is hidden in processed foods? One small can of chicken soup, for example, can contain well over half the recommended daily intake of salt for an adult, which is 6g (about 1 tsp). That's another reason why home-cooked food is so much better for you. You can add less salt, and even if you have been used to a salty diet, eventually you will have trained your taste buds to enjoy foods with less. Use herbs and spices to enhance the natural flavours of foods and before long you'll be enjoying the real taste of the food – not the flavour of salt.

Top ten tips for healthy eating

1   Enjoy your food.

2   Eat a variety of different foods – don't be tempted to stick to the same meals each week.

3   Eat the right amount to be a healthy weight. You can check this by using a Body Mass Index (BMI) calculator on the Internet.

4   Eat foods rich in carbohydrates and fibre and choose wholegrain cereals if you can. If you're putting on weight, keep carbohydrate portions smaller and increase your vegetables.

5   Eat at least five servings of fruit and vegetables each day.

6   Keep sugary foods and drinks, and food high in fat, as an occasional treat.

7   If you drink alcohol, stay within the guidelines: no more than 2 units of alcohol a day for women and no more than 3 units a day for men, with at least one alcohol-free day a week. One unit equals a standard measure of spirits, a half-pint of normal-strength beer or lager, or a small glass of wine.

8   Choose reduced- and low-fat dairy products when possible.

9   Aim to drink between six and eight glasses of water a day.

10 Avoid adding salt to food.

Your kitchen will have most of these four pieces of kit. Take a bit of time to learn how to use them – it will make life easier.

THE FRIDGE

Beware: the fridge is the main culprit for waste. It easily becomes a repository for out-of-date sauces and decomposing vegetable matter. Check the shelves and salad drawer regularly and use up foods before they become inedible. See page 13 for ways to use up odds and ends.

Your Fridge, Freezer, Microwave and Oven

TOP TEN FRIDGE KNOW-HOW TIPS

1   Put all perishable food in the fridge as soon as possible after purchase, checking all dates and storage instructions on the label.

2   Wrap or cover all food except most fruit and vegetables, but keep berries covered.

3   Keep pre-packed fresh meat in its original wrapping and use by the date shown. Unwrap freshly bought meat, put on a plate or dish and cover loosely with clingfilm or with a plate or upturned bowl, then put on a low shelf in the fridge. Don't allow it to drip on to other foods. Be especially careful with chicken, which can contain harmful bacteria (see page 21).

4   The coldest shelves are at the bottom of the fridge, so store raw meat, fish and poultry there.

5   To store fish, remove it from its original wrapping, rinse in cold water and pat dry, then cover with clingfilm or or with a plate or upturned bowl.

6   Always separate cooked meat and poultry from all raw foods and store it above them.

7   Store cheeses and eggs (in their egg boxes) on the top shelf.

8   Use the salad drawer for leafy and salad vegetables, carrots, courgettes, leeks and cauliflower, and so on, but do not store tomatoes, potatoes and bananas in the fridge, as they do not suit being stored in the cold.

9   Re-cover cream, yogurt and similar dairy foods once opened, as they will absorb other flavours.

10   Cool cooked food to room temperature before putting in the fridge.

THE FREEZER

Apart from storing the obvious frozen foods, you can also freeze sliced bread (toast it from frozen), portions of homemade soup, cartons of fresh soup (reheat from frozen) and bacon (but pack it in single rashers between sheets of baking parchment).

It's essential to allow frozen meat and poultry to thaw completely before cooking, so it's best to take it out of the freezer the night before and leave it in the fridge overnight. Put it on a plate to contain the drips. It will be ready to cook by the time you get home the next day. Cook food as soon as possible after thawing and ensure it's piping hot all the way through after cooking.

TOP FIVE FREEZER KNOW-HOW TIPS

1   Put frozen food in the freezer immediately you get home.

2   Freeze fresh food as soon as possible after purchase.

3   Never put warm foods into the freezer, wait until they have cooled, then chill in the fridge first.

4   Do not refreeze food once it has thawed.

5   Freeze raw or cooked food in portions – pack in freezer bags or plastic containers, preferably labelled with name and date.

How long can I store it?

Vegetables and fruit

Green vegetables	3–4 days
Salad leaves	2–3 days
Hard and stone fruit	3–7 days
Soft fruit	1–2 days

Dairy Food

Eggs and hard cheeses	1 week
Soft cheeses	2–3 days
Milk	4–5 days

Seafood

Fish and shellfish	1 day

Raw meat

Bacon	7 days
Joints and sausages	3 days
Minced meat and offal (liver, kidneys, etc.)	1 day
Chicken and raw sliced meat	2 days

Cooked meat

Joints	3 days
Casseroles, stews, pies, sliced meat and ham	2 days
Vacuum-packed ham	1–2 weeks
	(or as the pack instructions)

TO HELP THE FRIDGE WORK PROPERLY

- Don't overfill it.
- Don't put hot foods in it.
- Don't leave the door open.
- Keep it clean!

TO HELP THE FREEZER WORK PROPERLY

- Keep the freezer as full as possible.
- Never add foods that are still warm.
- Defrost it occasionally!

Don't try to freeze fried foods (which will go soggy), sauces made with egg, or whole eggs – but you can freeze whites and yolks separately.

THE MICROWAVE

You can use a microwave for scrambling eggs, cooking ready-prepared meals, vegetables and fish and for softening butter, and reheating foods and drinks. Use any microwave-proof plastic containers (ordinary plastic will buckle), ovenproof glass and ceramic dishes. Shallow, oval or round dishes are best for evenly cooked food. Choose light-coloured containers – dark ones can absorb too much heat, preventing the food from cooking properly.

TOP TEN MICROWAVE KNOW-HOW TIPS

1 Don't use metal containers, as the microwaves will bounce off the metal resulting in food that remains cold. This can also cause damage to the microwave oven.

2 Stir liquid food at least once during cooking, or turn large items of food over.

3 Allow food to rest for a few minutes before eating, to allow the heat to distribute evenly.

4 Cover fatty foods, such as bacon and sausages, with kitchen paper to soak up the fat.

5 Use a plastic trivet to help the underside of the food cook.

6 The microwave oven will work only if the door is closed. The door has a special seal to prevent microwaves, which are dangerous, from escaping.

7 Never switch on the microwave when there is nothing inside – the waves will bounce off the walls of the oven and could damage it.

8 Allow sufficient space around the microwave for ventilation through the air vents.

9 Don't use a microwave for browning meat, cooking puff pastry or breaded or battered foods.

10 Clean the interior and exterior from time to time.

THE OVEN

All ovens cook slightly differently but, generally, fan ovens produce a more even distribution of heat, so they cook food more quickly than conventional ovens. This means you need to adjust the cooking time or temperature for your recipe. The recipes in this book give you an alternative temperature for a fan oven, which is 20°C lower than for a conventional oven.

To cope with spills in the oven, line the bottom with aluminium foil (away from any electric element). Your oven may have a self-cleaning lining but parts will still need cleaning. Clean it occasionally!

REHEATING COOKED FOOD

When you reheat leftovers it's essential that they are thoroughly heated through and really piping hot. It's the only way to kill any bacteria, so be extra careful. Reheat food once only. Never keep cooked rice warm, as bacteria can develop. Serve it immediately.

Kitchen Sense

In any student house the kitchen is often a busy place and it's easy for it to become rather mucky and grimy if you don't try to clear up more or less as you go along. Although you don't need to become an obsessive cleaning freak, it's worth knowing some basic rules of food hygiene to keep yourself and your housemates safe.

KEEPING THE KITCHEN CLEAN

Thoroughly wipe down work surfaces after use, using clean soapy water. Rinse out the sink daily and wash it properly at least once a week. Don't let pieces of food or fat get washed down the sink, as they can block it – as well as making it smell. Allow fat to cool in the pan before disposing of it.

Empty the bin regularly and wash it out once a week (make sure you don't run out of bin liners). Sweep the floor regularly and wash it once a week. Replace washing-up sponges and brushes frequently and change the tea towels every couple of days; wash them with the washing up cloths at a high temperature. Keep all utensils and equipment clean.

TOP FIVE FOOD PREPARATION TIPS

1 Cleanliness while preparing food is essential, because poor hygiene puts you and others at risk of food poisoning.

2 Always wash your hands with soap, and scrub your nails, before and after handling food, and when handling different types of food.

3 Use one chopping board for raw meat, fish or poultry, and another for vegetables and cooked food.

4 Scrub chopping boards with hot, soapy water, then rinse with very hot, clean water.

5 Never put cooked or ready-to-eat food on a surface that has just had raw meat, chicken or fish on it – wash the surface thoroughly first.

Chicken

Raw poultry is the most risky food, because it can contain salmonella bacteria, which causes food poisoning, so take extra care in storing:

- Store pre-wrapped chicken in its original wrapping. Remove fresh chicken from its wrapping and make a note of the use-by date instructions on the label. Cook thoroughly within two days (see page 38).
- Freeze chicken on the day it is purchased. Freeze pre-wrapped chicken in its original wrapping. Remove fresh chicken from the wrapping, then re-wrap in a strong freezer bag, seal and date. It will keep for up to six months.

- To thaw a whole chicken, leave it in its wrapping, place on a large plate and put in the refrigerator for a minimum of 12 hours. Chicken joints will take less time. Use as soon as it has thawed. Never refreeze it once it has thawed.
- After you have prepared chicken, wash your hands and all preparation areas thoroughly, including the sink and especially the taps.

Shopping

It's all too easy to either buy what you don't need or forget to buy what you do need, so it's worth having some kind of routine before you go shopping. Always check your cupboards, fridge and freezer to ensure you stock up on basics that are running low and then give some thought about the week's meals so that you can get a list together of what you'll need.

Remember that there are only so many perishable items that you can actually eat in one week, so don't buy so many that there is little hope of you eating them before the use-by date. Select food carefully and buy it in optimum condition. That means, checking that the packaging is undamaged and that cans are not dented or bulging.

Although you can buy most produce all year round, it's going to taste better and – more importantly when eating on a budget – it will be much cheaper when it's in season. Also, if you want to shop ethically and avoid environmentally damaging food miles, look out for local produce which, of course, will be seasonal.

Top five shopping tips

1   Mostly stick to your shopping list and only buy special offers if you think you'll use them.

2   Buy seasonal foods.

3   If you have a freezer, buy larger amounts of meat or poultry and freeze portions, especially if they are on offer.

4   Compare the price per kilo. Loose fruit and vegetables can cost considerably less than pre-packed versions, for example.

5   Don't get carried away with the vegetables and fruit sections – only buy what you need for a week.

THINK DIFFERENTLY

One approach to shopping is to do a big supermarket shop once a month for non-perishables (including toiletries and other non-food items) and then buy the fresh ingredients weekly. You might even like to buy some items locally.

Be careful of special offers or BOGOFs (buy one, get one free). You don't always need them but, if you have time to cook in batches or you have space to freeze the extra, they might be useful. Avoid ready-meals and only buy ready-prepared ingredients if they are on a special offer – you'll be paying more for convenience.

BEFORE YOU GO SHOPPING

When you do your quick weekly stocktake of the storecupboard, fridge and freezer, see what ingredients are close to their use-by dates, then think about how they can be incorporated into the menus for the next few days. Don't forget the Thai curry sauce hiding at the back of the fridge – it needs to be used within a month, so plan a chicken or vegetable and nut curry to use it up. Look at the recipes in this book and see what you need to buy to make the date-challenged ingredients into something tasty.

PLAN YOUR MEALS FOR THE WEEK

It's well worth having an idea of what you intend to eat for each day of the following week. Include some dishes that you've already made and frozen. Think about meals that might be worth making in bulk – a chicken curry or a pasta sauce, for example. Or make a batch of basic Bolognese sauce and eat half one night then turn the remainder into a chilli with a can of red kidney beans and a few chilli flakes for the next night.

Don't forget to include vegetables and salads to accompany the dishes, but plan to have meals with salad earlier in the week rather than later, as it doesn't last as well as some other vegetables. Bear in mind that you may want to change your plan if you find a bargain in the supermarket.

Rethink your approach to cooking – meat and fish are expensive, so make two nights a week vegetarian.

MAKE READY-MADE FOODS WORK FOR YOU

The deli counters and canned goods shelves can provide you with the ingredients to whip up instant meals for when you're exceptionally rushed, but you'll need to shop wisely – some of these items can work out expensive.

- Buy some good-quality stir-fry, pasta or cook-in sauces. You just need to pop the meat, chicken or prawns in the pan with it and cook it through.
- Use ready-baked pastry cases to make a quick flan, for a change.
- Top a bought pizza base with your own healthy ingredients.
- See what the deli counter can offer to go with a salad or to top a pizza: marinated vegetables, cold meats, cured fish and cheeses.

If you've never followed a recipe before, you'll find it's actually quite easy, because the instructions will take you through step by step. It's worth choosing a simple recipe for your first try, however. A sauce made with meat and vegetables or a curry using a curry paste, for example, are fairly simple for the novice cook.

Get Down to Some Cooking

FIRST THINGS FIRST

- Read the recipe through quickly to make sure you understand it and have enough time to make it. Check how many it serves and amend the quantities accordingly, if the recipe is suitable, if you are cooking for one.

- Check that you have all the necessary ingredients, then make a list of anything that you need to buy (but see the Recipe Shortcuts box opposite). Sometimes you can create a good meal without including every single ingredient listed.

- Check that you have the pans and other equipment.

- Before you start cooking, clear the decks in the kitchen to give yourself room to work.

- If the oven needs to be preheated it will say so in step 1 of the recipe, so do that first.

- The ingredients in a recipe are listed in order of use. It's not necessary to weigh and prepare everything in one go first. You can prepare the onions, say, for the first step and while they're cooking for 5 minutes prepare the next group of vegetables or trim and cube the meat. But if you're cooking a stir-fry you will need to prepare all the ingredients in one go, as it's a very fast cooking method.

- The recipe method will take you through each stage step by step. Take your time at each step before moving on to the next one.

- Use a timer if you have one, or the alarm on your mobile phone – once something is in the oven or bubbling on the hob, it's easy to get distracted and lose track of time.

- Stay in the kitchen while cooking – a pan full of hot fat can be dangerous if it flares up while you've gone walkabout.

- Clear up as you go along.

Top five recipe shortcuts

1 Don't bother with the garnishes.

2 Do use dried herbs instead of fresh if they are being cooked in the dish, but if they are to be added at the end they need to be fresh. Coriander and parsley always need to be fresh, though. (Parsley is cheaper and both herbs can be frozen to avoid waste – dry the leaves, pack into a freezer bag and label. To use, crumble from frozen into the dishes.)

3 If you've only got a green pepper when it should be red, it's OK to use, but the flavour will be slightly different.

4 If you don't have all the vegetables listed, just increase the ones you do have.

5 If you only ever keep mixed herbs, you can use these instead of the specified herb, but the dish won't taste exactly as the recipe – and all your dishes will taste rather similar.

Is it cooked?

It's important that food is cooked through thoroughly, especially chicken. Always check that chicken is cooked by cutting it through its thickest part (into the thick part of the leg, if cooking a roast or a chicken portion). The juices should run clear with no pink juices. Beef and lamb can be eaten pink; pork must be cooked through.

Kitchen fires – what to do

Most fires that occur in the kitchen begin when a chip pan or frying pan bursts into flames. Do not leave a pan unattended when frying.

NEVER put water on to fat that is burning; it can cause an explosion.

1 Leave the pan where it is.

2 Turn off the heat, if it is safe to do so.

3 Protect your hands, then put a damp cloth (such as a tea towel), a close-fitting lid or a fire blanket over the pan to smother the flames.

4 Allow the pan to cool for at least 30 minutes. (The fire can start again if the cover is removed too soon.)

Ideally, use a thermostatically controlled deep-fat fryer rather than an ordinary hob-top chip pan, as it is very easy for fat to become too hot and then to burst into flames.

A smoke alarm (to BS 5446) is well worth fitting to the kitchen ceiling or hallway just outside.

The Basics

Basic Sauces and Dressings

Eggs

Cheese

Poultry and Meat

Fish

Vegetables

Pasta and Noodles

Rice, Grains and Pulses

Stir-frying

Herbs and Spices

Basic Sauces and Dressings

Gravy

A rich gravy is great served with roast chicken and meat. If possible, make the gravy in the roasting tin after the chicken or meat is cooked and you've taken it out of the tin to rest (this allows the juices to settle and the meat to be tender). This will incorporate the meat juices that have escaped during roasting.

To make 300ml ($^1/_2$ pint):

1 Carefully pour (or skim) off the fat from a corner of the roasting tin, leaving the sediment behind. Put the tin on the hob over a medium heat and pour in 300–450ml (10–15fl oz) vegetable water, or chicken, vegetable or meat stock, as appropriate.

2 Stir thoroughly, scraping up the sediment and boil steadily until the gravy is a rich brown colour.

Or try...

Thick gravy
Sprinkle 1–2 tbsp plain flour into the roasting tin and cook, stirring, until browned, then gradually stir in the liquid and cook, stirring, for 2–3 minutes until smooth and slightly thickened.

Sauces

White sauce

Use as a base for lasagne or fish pie, or stir in grated cheese, mustard or herbs and use as a sauce for fish or chicken.

To make 300ml (¹/₂ pint), you will need:
15g (½oz) butter
15g (½oz) plain flour
300ml (½ pint) milk
freshly grated nutmeg

1 Melt the butter in a pan, stir in the flour and cook, stirring, for 1 minute until cooked but not coloured. (This is called a roux.)

2 Remove from the heat and gradually pour in the milk, whisking all the time. Season lightly with salt, pepper and nutmeg.

3 Put the pan back on the heat and cook, stirring constantly, until the sauce is thick and smooth. Simmer gently for 2 minutes.

Or try...

Cheese sauce
Take the pan off the heat and stir 50g (2oz) finely grated Cheddar or Gruyère cheese and a large pinch of mustard powder or cayenne pepper into the finished sauce. Heat gently to melt the cheese. Use for Cauliflower Cheese or Macaroni Cheese (see pages 254, 166).

Parsley sauce
Stir in 2 tbsp freshly chopped parsley at step 3.

To make cheese sauce in the microwave
Pour the milk into a measuring jug or microwaveable bowl. Add the butter and flour and whisk to combine. The butter won't mix in, but don't worry. Microwave on full power (based on a 900W oven) for 2 minutes, then remove and whisk together. Cook for another 2 minutes and whisk again. The sauce should be thick and smooth. Season well, then add the cheese and mustard or pepper and stir until melted.

3

✓ Top Tip
Quick and easy white sauce
Blend 1 tbsp cornflour with 2 tbsp cold water until smooth. Warm 300ml (½ pint) milk in a pan then stir in the cornflour mixture. Bring to the boil, stirring constantly for 2–3 minutes to thicken and cook through.

THE BASICS

Salad dressings

⟳ Swap

Instead of extra virgin olive oil, use olive oil.

French dressing

1 tsp Dijon mustard
a pinch of sugar
1 tbsp red or white wine vinegar
6 tbsp extra virgin olive oil
salt and ground black pepper

1 Put the mustard, sugar and vinegar into a small bowl and season with salt and pepper. Whisk until well combined, then gradually whisk in the oil until thoroughly combined.

2 Store in a cool place if not using immediately. Whisk briefly before using.

Or try...

Garlic dressing

Add 1 crushed garlic clove to the dressing with the mustard, sugar and vinegar.

Balsamic dressing

Put 2 tbsp balsamic vinegar and 4 tbsp extra virgin olive oil into a small bowl and whisk to combine. Season with salt and ground black pepper.

Fresh herb dressing

Put ½ tsp Dijon mustard, a pinch of sugar and 1 tbsp lemon juice into a bowl and season with salt and ground black pepper. Whisk until well combined, then gradually whisk in 6 tbsp extra virgin olive oil until thoroughly combined. Stir in 2 tbsp freshly chopped herbs, such as parsley, chives and chervil.

Dijon mustard

Put 2 tbsp vinegar, 4 tbsp olive oil and 1½ tsp Dijon mustard into a small bowl and whisk to combine. Season with salt and ground black pepper.

Eggs

Apart from boiling them whole, eggs need to be either cracked open, separated into white and yolks, or whisked – and once you have mastered these simple techniques you will be able to cook eggs in lots of different ways.

Cracking and separating

You'll need to separate eggs for some recipes. It's easy, but it requires care. If you're separating more than one egg, break each one into an individual cup. Separating them individually means that if you break one yolk, you won't spoil the whole batch. Keeping the whites yolk-free is particularly important if you need to whisk them.

1. Crack the egg more carefully than usual: right in the middle to make a break between the two halves that is just wide enough to get your thumbnail into.

2. Holding the egg over a bowl with the large end pointing down, carefully lift off the small half. Some of the white will drip and slide into the bowl while the yolk sits in the large end of the shell.

3. Carefully slide the yolk into the smaller end, then back into the large end to allow the remaining white to drop into the bowl. Take care not to break the yolk; even a speck can stop the whites from whisking up.

Whisking

1. Use a hand whisk or electric whisk. Make sure that there is no trace of yolk in the whites and that the whisk and bowl are clean and dry. At a low speed, use the whisk in a small area of the whites until it starts to become foamy.

2. Increase the speed and work the whisk through the whites until glossy and soft rounded peaks form. Do not over-whisk, as the foam will become dry and grainy.

Cooking eggs

How to fry an egg

1 Crack an egg into a bowl or cup, so that if some of the shell falls in you can scoop it out with a teaspoon.

2 Heat 1 tbsp vegetable or sunflower oil in a non-stick frying pan for 1 minute. If you don't have a non-stick pan use 3 tbsp oil.

3 Turn the heat down low and carefully pour the egg into the hot fat. (If the heat is too high, the white will burn before the yolk is cooked.) Tilt the pan and use a large spoon to scoop fat up and pour it over the yolk – this cooks the yolk at the same time as the white.

4 Cook until the yolk is just set.

How to poach an egg

1 Fill a deep frying pan two-thirds full with water and bring to the boil.

2 Break an egg on to a saucer and slide carefully into the water.

3 Using a large metal spoon, gently roll the egg over two or three times to wrap the white around the yolk. Take the pan off the heat, cover and leave to stand for 3 minutes. Serve immediately. Use a slotted spoon to remove the egg from the pan.

How to boil an egg

Bring a small pan of water to the boil. Once the water is boiling, add a medium egg. For a soft-boiled egg, cook for 6 minutes and for hard-boiled, cook for 10 minutes. Using a slotted spoon, remove the egg from the hot water and serve.

Scrambled eggs

1 Beat 2 medium eggs in a bowl lightly with a fork. Season with salt and ground black pepper.

2 Melt a knob of butter in a small pan over a low heat and pour in the eggs.

3 Start stirring immediately, to break up the lumps as they form and keep the eggs moving while cooking. When they are the consistency you prefer – soft or firmer – remove from the heat.

To scramble eggs in the microwave

Put all the ingredients into a bowl and beat well. Cook at full power for 1 minute (the mixture should be just starting to set around the edges). Beat again. Cook at full power for 2–3 minutes, stirring every 30 seconds, until cooked to your liking.

Baked eggs

1 Preheat the oven – see step 3. Generously smear individual baking dish(es) or one large baking dish with butter.

2 Put in any accompaniments, if using (see below). If using a vegetable-based accompaniment, use the back of a spoon to make a hollow or hollows in it in which to break the egg or eggs. Carefully crack the egg or eggs into the hollows.

3 Bake for 8–10 minutes at 200°C (180°C fan oven) mark 6, or 15–18 minutes at 180°C (160°C fan oven) mark 4, until the whites are just set; the yolks should still be quite runny.

✅ Top Tips

- Accompaniments must be fully cooked before they are transferred to the baking dish and the raw eggs put on top.
- Eggs are delicious baked on top of sautéed vegetables – such as ratatouille (see page 259), lightly browned diced potatoes with onions, and well-cooked spinach.
- If you like, drizzle a small spoonful of cream and a good grinding of black pepper on top of the eggs before baking.

Perfect omelettes
- Beat the eggs lightly.
- Use a small frying pan – 18cm (7in) is ideal.
- Use a high heat.
- Don't add butter until the pan is already hot, otherwise it will become overbrown.

Making omelettes

There are numerous different types of omelette – from the folded omelette made from simple beaten eggs to thick omelettes such as Spanish tortilla and Italian frittata.

To serve 1, you will need:
15g (½oz) butter
2 medium eggs, beaten
salt and ground black pepper

1 Add the butter to a preheated small frying pan and let it sizzle for a few moments without browning, then pour in the beaten eggs and stir a few times with a fork.

2 As the omelette begins to stick at the sides of the pan, lift it up and let the uncooked egg run into the gap.

3 When the omelette is nearly set and the underneath is brown, loosen the edges and give the pan a sharp shake to slide the omelette across.

4 Add a filling (such as grated cheese or fried mushrooms) if you like, and fold the far side of the omelette towards you. Tilt the pan to slide the omelette on to the plate and serve.

Or try...

Ham
Chop 50g (2oz) ham and sprinkle over the eggs as soon as you've added them to the pan.

Herb
Add 1 tsp each finely chopped chives and tarragon, or 1 tbsp chopped parsley, to the beaten egg mixture before cooking.

Tomato
Fry 2 skinned and chopped tomatoes in a little butter for 5 minutes or until soft and pulpy. Put in the centre of the omelette before folding.

Cheese
Grate 40g (1½oz) Cheddar cheese. Sprinkle half on the omelette before folding. Sprinkle the rest over the finished omelette.

Mushroom
Thickly slice 50g (2oz) mushrooms and cook in butter until soft. Put in the centre of the omelette before folding.

To make 8 pancakes, you will need:

125g (4oz) plain flour
a pinch of salt
1 medium egg
300ml (½ pint) milk
oil and butter to fry

1 Sift the flour and salt into a bowl, make a well in the middle and whisk in the egg. Work in the milk, then leave to stand for 20 minutes.

2 Heat a pan and coat lightly with oil or butter. Pour just a little batter into the pan and swirl to coat the bottom of the pan.

3 Cook for 1½–2 minutes until golden, carefully turning once. Remove from the pan on to a warmed plate, and repeat with the remaining batter.

€ Moneysaver Tip

Use half milk and half water if you don't have enough milk.

Savoury pancake fillings

Almost any mixture of cooked vegetables, fish or chicken, flavoured with herbs and moistened with a little soured cream or cream cheese can be used. Try the following – just spoon on to the pancake, fold over and serve:

1 Mix 25g (1oz) each grated cheese and chopped ham with 1 tbsp crème fraîche (or use mayonnaise).

2 Ratatouille (see page 259).

3 Sautéed spinach, pinenuts and feta cheese.

4 Smoked haddock and chopped hard-boiled egg with soured cream.

✔ Top Tip
How can I tell if my eggs are fresh?

A fresh egg should feel heavy in your hand and will sink to the bottom of the bowl or float on its side when put into water. Older eggs, over two weeks old, will float vertically.

THE BASICS

Cheese

Main types of cheese

Cheddar

Cheddar is a hard English cheese, traditionally made from unpasteurised cow's milk. Smoked versions, including applewood and charnwood, are available. It's good for cooking as it grates and melts well.

Parmesan

Parmesan is a cooked, pressed cheese with a distinctive flavour that sharpens with age. Parmesan is sold whole or in wedges. Ready-grated Parmesan is a cheaper option but is not as tasty as a piece of the cheese. Parmesan grates and melts well; add the scraped rind to soups, stock or sauces.

Gruyère

The most famous of Swiss cheeses, Gruyère has a distinctive and fairly sweet taste – at first fruity, then more earthy and nutty. The natural rust-coloured brown rind is hard and dry, the inside is pale yellow, with a dense, compact texture dotted irregularly with peasized holes. It's an excellent cooking cheese – use in sauces, bakes, soups and fondues.

Feta

This soft, unpressed fresh Greek cheese is a pure-white rindless cheese, made in blocks using animal rennet, and stored in brine, where it will keep almost indefinitely. It has a sharp, salty taste and a crumbly texture. Use in salads, in pastries and pies or sprinkled on to stews.

Cream cheese

Cream cheese is made from a mixture of cream and pasteurised milk. It has a mildly acid flavour, a rather granular texture, and a buttery consistency that makes it easy to spread. Cream cheese should be eaten shortly after opening or within a day or two of purchase if bought from a large tub. Use as a spread, in baking and desserts, and as a frosting for cakes; and in sauces, savoury dishes and dips.

Mascarpone

Not technically a cheese, as it is made from matured cream, mascarpone is often described as a cream cheese. It has a soft texture, a creamy, mild flavour, and a fat content of 75 per cent. Serve as an alternative to cream with fresh fruit, as a cake filling or topping, or in sauces.

Mozzarella

This fresh cheese, traditionally made from buffalo milk, is now often made with cow's milk. Pasteurised milk is curdled and formed into balls, which are stored in their own water or whey. Older mozzarella, sold in blocks, can be rubbery but melts to form a stringy, chewy cheese, often used on pizzas. Mozzarella should be

stored in its own whey or water in the fridge and used within a few days of opening. Use young mozzarella in salads, older mozzarella in pizzas and lasagnes.

Halloumi

Another fresh cheese, this Cypriot cheese is a traditional semi-hard sheep's milk cheese flavoured with mint. It has a milky, salty taste and a rubbery texture. Halloumi is sometimes made with goat's milk or cow's milk. It is always

served cooked, usually by grilling, griddling or frying until the exterior is browned and slightly crisped. It is often found in Middle Eastern dishes – cubed and grilled on skewers with slices of vegetables and served with pitta bread and hummus.

Gorgonzola

One of the blue cheeses, this is a creamy-textured Italian cheese. There are two styles: dolce, or nuovo, is soft, creamy and smelly; naturale or picante is more crumbly, firmer, and

stronger in flavour. Use in salads, dips and dressings. In cooking, add to soups, pasta sauces or risottos.

Cooking with cheese

The less cooking cheese has, the better. Overheating tends to make it tough and indigestible, so when making a dish such as cheese sauce, always heat the cheese very gently and do not cook longer than is necessary to melt it. Most hard cheeses are excellent for grating and melting. Soft cheeses won't grate, but can be used baked or melted into sauces. Semi-soft cheeses are excellent for grilling. Blue cheeses are good for melting into sauces, or crumbling into salads. Fresh cheeses such as halloumi (see left) can be sliced and pan-fried, griddled or grilled.

How to choose cheese

Avoid any cheese that has a strong ammonia odour. Hard or semi-hard cheese that has beads of moisture on the surface, or a dry, cracked rind, should be rejected. Semi-soft cheeses should yield to gentle pressure and any powdery bloom on the rind should be evenly coloured and slightly moist.

Buy only as much as you need (even if it's just a sliver) for consumption within a few days. Refrigeration at home will dry out the cheese.

If buying pre-packed cheese, check that it does not look sweaty or excessively runny and that it is within the life of its date stamp. If the date is many weeks ahead, it may mean that the cheese is immature; this may not matter if you intend to serve the cheese at this immature stage or to store it for using when mature.

Vegetarian cheeses

Some vegetarians prefer to avoid cheeses that have been produced by the traditional method, because this uses animal-derived rennet. Most supermarkets and cheese shops now stock an excellent range of vegetarian cheeses, produced using vegetarian rennet.

THE BASICS

37

Poultry and Meat

Buying and storing chicken

Most chickens from the butcher or supermarket are sold ready for the oven. Look for birds with no signs of damage or blemishes. If the birds are not wrapped in plastic, check that they smell pleasant. Generally, the larger the bird, the greater proportion of meat to bone there will be – and therefore better value. Check that the birds have a neat shape, an even colour and no bruises or tears on the skin. The body should look meaty and plump.

Some whole birds are bought with a packet of giblets (neck, liver, heart and crop) tucked inside the carcass. Remove and store them in a sealed container in the fridge, to use within a day. Put the bird in a shallow dish, cover with clingfilm and store in the fridge. Use within two days, or according to the 'use-by' date on its label. Poultry from the supermarket can be left in its original packaging.

✅ Top Tip

Look in the freezer aisle of the supermarket for packs of frozen chicken breasts and thighs. They're usually smaller fillets but cheaper as a result and make a good stand-by.

See page 21 for hygiene notes when handling chicken.

How to freeze and thaw chicken

You can safely freeze fresh uncooked chicken but be sure to follow the guidelines below:

- Always freeze poultry before its 'use-by' date, preferably on the day of purchase.

- Follow any freezing or thawing instructions given.

- Wrap portions in individual freezer bags, seal tightly and label with the date of freezing. They can be stored in the freezer for up to three months.

- To thaw, put the poultry in a dish (to catch dripping juices) and leave overnight in the fridge until completely thawed, then cook within 24 hours.

- Do not re-freeze thawed poultry. You can, however, freeze it again after you have cooked it.

Roasting a chicken

Don't be put off by the idea of roasting – a roasted chicken is easy to cook and very economical.

Easy roast chicken

To serve 4–6, you will need:
1.8kg (4lb) chicken
25g (1oz) butter, softened
2 tbsp olive oil
1 lemon, cut in half
1 small head of garlic, unpeeled,
    cut in half horizontally
salt and ground black pepper
roast potatoes (see page 56) and vegetables to serve

1   Preheat the oven to 220°C (200°C fan oven) mark 7. Put the chicken into a roasting tin just large enough to hold it comfortably. Spread the butter all over the chicken, then drizzle with the oil and season with salt and pepper.

2   Squeeze the lemon juice over the chicken, then put one lemon half inside the chicken. Put the other half and the garlic into the roasting tin.

3   Put the chicken into the oven for 15 minutes, then turn the heat down to 190°C (170°C fan oven) mark 5 and cook for a further 45 minutes–1 hour until the leg juices run clear when pierced with a sharp knife. Baste from time to time with the pan juices. Add a splash of water to the tin if the juices dry out.

4   Put the chicken on a warm plate, cover with foil and leave to 'rest' for 10 minutes, so that the juices settle back into the meat, making it moist and easier to slice. Mash some of the garlic into the pan juices and serve the gravy with the chicken, with potatoes and vegetables.

 Top Tip
Use any leftover roast chicken in lunches, salads and stir-fries, soups, curries and wraps.

Timesaver Tip
Set the alarm on your mobile phone, or use a timer, and let the oven do the work while you get on with other things.

THE BASICS

Poaching chicken

This gentle method of cooking will produce a light broth.

1 Brown the bird in oil if you like (this is not necessary but will give a deeper flavour), then transfer to a pan that will hold it easily: a large pan or frying pan is good for pieces, a flameproof casserole for a whole bird.

2 Add 1 roughly peeled and chopped onion, 2 crushed garlic cloves, 2 peeled and chopped carrots, 2 chopped celery sticks, 6 whole black peppercorns and 1 tsp dried mixed herbs. Pour in just enough stock to cover, then simmer on the hob, uncovered, for 30–40 minutes (for pieces) or about 1 hour (for a whole chicken).

3 Gently lift the bird out of the liquid. If you like, you can increase the heat under the pan to reduce the liquid a little – this will give you a stronger flavoured broth.

Instant flavour ideas for chicken

- Snip bacon into a frying pan, cook until crisp and golden, then stir into warm, boiled new potatoes with shredded cooked roast chicken and mustard mayonnaise. Serve with green salad.

- Roast a chicken with lots of tarragon, peppers, whole garlic cloves and olive oil. Serve with couscous, into which you've stirred the roasting juices.

- Marinate chicken thighs in olive oil with rosemary, thyme and crushed garlic (see page 51). Pan-fry the chicken thighs (see opposite). Serve with a Quick Tomato Sauce (see page 154).

Pan-frying chicken

This is a quick method for cooking smaller chicken or meat pieces and you can make a sauce with the pan juices at the end, if you like.

1 Put in enough oil to fill a frying pan to a depth of about 5mm (¼ in) and put the pan over a medium heat on the hob.

2 Season chicken pieces with salt and ground black pepper, then carefully add to the pan, flesh side down, and fry for 10–15 minutes until it's browned. (Don't put too many pieces of chicken in the pan at once or the chicken will cook partly in its own steam.)

3 Turn the pieces over and cook on the skin side for another 10–15 minutes until the skin is brown and the flesh is cooked, with no pink juices, but still moist all the way through.

4 Remove the chicken from the pan using a pair of tongs and keep warm. Pour off the excess oil from the pan, then add a little stock to the pan and stir to dislodge any bits on the bottom. Stir thoroughly, scraping up the sediment, then add some herbs and finely chopped garlic or onion and cook for a few minutes. Serve the chicken with the sauce.

Grilling chicken

This method is good for cooking tender pieces of chicken, or for strips or chunks threaded on to skewers.

1 Preheat the grill. Brush the chicken pieces with a flavoured oil. Put the pieces on a wire rack over a grill pan or roasting tin and set the pan under the grill so that it is about 8cm (3¼ in) from the heat source.

2 Every few minutes brush a teaspoon of the oil over the chicken.

3 When cooked on one side, turn with tongs and cook the other side until cooked through. Avoid piercing the flesh when turning. Allow 12–20 minutes – it is important that chicken is cooked all the way through: pierce with a sharp knife, the juices should run clear.

✔ Top Tips

- Don't rush the cooking by using a very high heat. If you need to speed things up, cover the pan during the first half of cooking.
- Don't let the chicken cook for too long, as it can quickly dry out and toughen over high heat.

Grilling times

Turn the chicken two or three times during cooking.

Kebabs	8–12 minutes
Thighs	10–15 minutes
Breast fillet	10–20 minutes

Pot-roasting chicken

Pot-roasting is a great way to cook chicken for when friends come round. There are just a couple of things to watch:

- Make sure that you use a large enough casserole and that the bird isn't too close to the sides of the dish.

- Check the liquid level in the casserole from time to time. If it's too dry, add a little more. Water is fine; stock or wine is even better.

Pot-roasted chicken

To serve 4–6, you will need:
2 tbsp vegetable oil
1 onion, peeled and cut into wedges
2 rindless streaky bacon rashers, chopped
1.4–1.6kg (3–3½ lb) chicken
6 carrots, halved
1 garlic clove, peeled and crushed
bouquet garni (see below) or 2 tsp dried mixed herbs
600ml (1 pint) chicken stock (see Top Tip)
100ml (3½ fl oz) dry white wine, if you have it
small handful of parsley, chopped
salt and ground black pepper

1   Preheat the oven to 200°C (180°C fan oven) mark 6. Heat the oil in a flameproof casserole. Fry the onion and bacon for 5 minutes, then remove from the pan and put onto a plate. Add the chicken to the casserole and brown it all over for 10 minutes, then remove from the pan and put on to the plate. Fry the carrots and garlic for 2 minutes, then add the bacon, onion and chicken.

2   Add the bouquet garni or herbs, stock, wine, if you have it, and season with salt and pepper. Bring to the boil, then transfer to the oven. Cook, basting now and then, for 1 hour 20 minutes or until the juices run clear. Carefully lift out the chicken – tip any liquid inside the bird back into the casserole. Stir the parsley into the liquid and carve the chicken.

Bouquet garni
This is a small bunch of herbs tied together with string, and an essential flavouring for stocks, soups and stews. The herbs can vary but usually include parsley, thyme and bay leaf; spices such as peppercorns and cloves may also be included. You remove it after cooking.

✅ Top Tip
You can use 1 chicken stock cube dissolved in 600ml (1 pint) boiling water.

🕐 Timesaver Tip
Set the alarm on your mobile phone, or use a timer, and let the oven do the work while you get on with other things.

Buying and storing meat

When buying meat, always check it carefully first: it should look and smell fresh. The flesh should look moist but not watery, and pink, red or dark red according to variety (mature beef will be dark red). Fat should be pale, creamy and firm – avoid meat where the fat is crumbly, waxy or yellowing. Look for meat that has been well cut and neatly trimmed and remember that some fat will add flavour.

Meat should be wrapped and stored in the fridge, placed in a dish so that if any juices escape they cannot drip and contaminate other foods. Do not allow the meat to touch any other foods. Raw meat can generally be stored for three to five days, although offal and minced or processed meat such as sausages can deteriorate more quickly and should be used within two days. Meat that is bought sealed in a pack can be stored in the fridge unopened, making sure that it is eaten before the use-by-date.

✅ Top Tip

You need smaller quantities when buying cuts of meat off the bone: allow 100–150g (3½–5oz) per person. For meat on the bone, allow slightly more, anything from 175–350g (6–12oz) per person depending on the cut.

How to freeze and thaw meat

You can safely freeze fresh uncooked meat but be sure to follow the guidelines below:

● Always freeze meat before its 'use-by' date, preferably on the day of purchase.

● Follow any freezing or thawing instructions given.

● Wrap portions in individual freezer bags, seal tightly and label with the date of freezing. They can be stored in the freezer for up to three months.

● To thaw, put the meat in a dish (to catch any dripping juices) and put in the fridge until completely thawed. Cook within two days.

● Do not refreeze raw meat that has thawed. You can, however, freeze it again after you have cooked it.

Braising and pot-roasting meat

- Good cuts of beef include shin, chuck, blade, brisket and flank; good cuts of lamb include leg, shoulder, neck, breast and shank; good cuts of pork include shoulder, hand, spring, belly and loin.
- Always use a low heat and check regularly to make sure that there is enough liquid to keep the meat from catching on the casserole.
- Braises often improve by being cooked in advance and then gently reheated before serving. If you've braised a whole piece of meat, you can slice it before reheating.

Braised meat

To serve 6, you will need:
3 tbsp olive oil
1.1kg (2½ lb) meat, cut into large chunks (see Moneysaver Tip)
1 large onion, peeled and thickly sliced
3 carrots, peeled and thickly sliced
3 celery sticks, thickly sliced
2 garlic cloves, peeled and crushed
2 x 400g cans chopped tomatoes
150ml (¼ pint) water or white wine
2 bay leaves
salt and ground black pepper

1 Preheat the oven to 170°C (150°C fan oven) mark 3. Heat the oil in a large flameproof casserole and lightly brown the meat all over, in two or three batches. Remove from the pan and put on to a plate. Add the onion, carrots, celery and garlic to the pan and cook until beginning to colour, then add the meat, tomatoes and water or wine.

2 Stir well, season and add the bay leaves. Bring to the boil, then cover the pan and transfer to the oven for 2 hours or until tender. Skim off any fat.

🕐 Timesaver Tip

Set the alarm on your mobile phone, or use a timer, and let the oven do the work while you get on with other things.

£ Moneysaver Tip

Meat is expensive, but if you get one of the cheaper cuts – like shin of beef – this will be an economical meal for six of you.

Pan-frying meat

1. Ideal for chops or steaks. Preheat a frying pan and season the meat with salt.

2. Pour in enough vegetable oil to coat the base of the pan. Put in the meat without crowding. Do not move it for at least the first minute of cooking – it may stick.

3. When the meat is well browned, turn and cook on the other side.

Grilling meat

1. Preheat the grill to high while you dry the meat with kitchen paper. Put the meat on a wire rack in the grill pan. If it has not been marinated, salt lightly.

2. Put the grill pan under the heat. Thin cuts should be about 2.5cm (1in) from the heat source, thicker cuts about 7.5cm (3in). Cook according to the table below.

Grilling times

Cut	Rare	Medium	Well done
Beef fillet	3–5 minutes	6–7 minutes	8–10 minutes
Other beefsteaks	5–6 minutes	8–12 minutes	15–18 minutes
Pork chops/steaks	8–10 minutes	10–14 minutes	
Lamb chops/steaks	8–10 minutes	10–14 minutes	
Lamb cutlets	6–10 minutes	8–12 minutes	

Note
Cooking times are approximate, for a piece of meat 2.5cm (1in) thick.

THE BASICS

Fish

Buying and storing fish

For the best results, fish should be as fresh as possible. It's often hard to tell in the supermarket how fresh a piece of fish is but there are some key signs to look for. A really fresh fish will have:

- An even covering of scales with no patches and no damage to the fins.

- Glossy taut skin.

- Bright and clear eyes and bright red gills.

- Flesh that feels firm rather than soft and spongy.

- Individual fillets should be moist, shiny and plump.

Fillets and steaks should:

- Be moist, shiny and plump.

- Show no signs of dryness or discoloration.

- Not look wet, shiny or slimy.

Fish is always best eaten fresh. So store it in the fridge when you get home, and cook it that day.

Frozen fish
Fish sold frozen is usually snap-frozen shortly after it is caught, and is generally of good quality. It is usually prepared as fillets and is used in processed products, such as fish fingers and fishcakes. Many types of fish and processed foods can be cooked directly from frozen and it will say this on the packet. Other frozen fish should be thawed according to the pack instructions and cooked as for fresh fish.

Preparing and cooking fish

Whole fish often need to be gutted and cleaned before cooking (except whitebait and red mullet). Those with tough scales should have the scales removed. Small to medium-sized fish can be cooked whole, whereas medium-large fish may be filleted or cut into steaks or chunks. Fillets and steaks may be cooked with the skin on or off, but skin should be removed before cutting the flesh into chunks or cubes. You can ask the fishmonger to clean, scale and skin the fish.

Different fish suit different cooking techniques. The main techniques are steaming, pan-frying, searing, grilling and baking. Fish cooks very quickly, and overcooking will ruin it, so follow the recipe.

How to freeze and thaw fish

- Fish can be frozen whole or in fillets, cutlets or steaks. Freeze as soon as possible after purchase.

- Gut and clean the fish or ask the fishmonger to do this. Pat dry on kitchen paper, then snip off any sharp fins or spikes.

- Wrap fish or fillets individually in clingfilm or a freezer bag, making sure the wrapping is airtight. Label with the date and store in the freezer. Use within two to three months.

- To thaw, place the fish in the fridge until completely thawed. This may take 24 hours for a large fish.

- Do not refreeze thawed raw fish. You can, however, freeze it again after you have cooked it.

Braising fish

For best results:

- Choose thick, fairly firm-fleshed fish if you are cooking it in pieces.
- You can choose a variety of vegetables and herbs to use in braised dishes: in the recipe below, try adding chopped red pepper and using oregano instead of thyme. Make sure that all the other ingredients are cooked and their flavours well developed before you add the fish.
- Once you add the fish to the pan, don't move it about too much as the flesh can easily break up. Be careful when removing it from the pan.

Braised fish

To serve 4, you will need:
1 tbsp oil
15g (½oz) butter
1 onion, peeled and chopped
2 garlic cloves, peeled and crushed
2 tbsp each freshly chopped parsley and thyme
400g can chopped tomatoes
about 900g (2lb) firm-fleshed fish, such as pollack, hake and whiting

1 Put the oil and butter into a large frying pan and cook the onion and garlic until soft. Add the herbs and tomatoes to the pan and cook until the tomatoes are fairly thick.

2 Put the fish on the vegetables and spoon the tomatoes over it.

3 Cook for 5–10 minutes until the fish is just cooked through.

 Moneysaver Tip
Make this when you see some cheap fish on sale.

Everyday fish

Cod

Once plentiful,
cod has been
over-fished and stocks have

dropped to dangerously low levels. Cod is usually available as steaks or fillets. Cod suits simple flavourings such as butter and lemon, or sauces such as parsley or a creamy cheese sauce, as well as Mediterranean flavours. Batter and deep-fry, braise in sauces, poach, grill, bake or roast. Avoid overcooking, as the flesh easily becomes dry or watery.

Pollack

Pollack is a member of the cod family with firm, white, flavoursome flesh. Although usually considered inferior to cod and haddock in flavour, its abundance and lower price make it a good alternative. Pollack is usually sold as fillets or cutlets. It goes well with Indian spices such as cumin, coriander and turmeric, as well as Mediterranean flavours. Braise, bake or add to soups, casseroles and fish pies.

Whiting

Whiting is one of the smallest members of the cod family, and has delicately flavoured flesh. It is usually sold whole. Less expensive than cod, it is good cooked with garlic, tomatoes and dill, or a citrus sauce. Pan-fry or grill whole fish. Deep-fry, braise or poach fillets, or add to soups.

Hake

Hake is
another

member of the cod family, and similarly over-fished. Their flesh is white and fragile with a delicate flavour, and should be cooked with care. Hake is usually available as steaks and cutlets and goes well with garlic and white wine, tomatoes and paprika. Poach, braise, bake or fry.

Mackerel

Mackerel
can vary
greatly in
size but

the average fish weighs about 450g (1lb). The flesh is a beige-pink and has a meaty texture and rich flavour. Mackerel are in plentiful supply and inexpensive, and are excellent in terms of price:quality ratio. They are usually sold whole and are best eaten very fresh. Serve well seasoned with pepper and grilled, with just a squeeze of lemon juice, or accompany with a sharp and piquant sauce such as gooseberry, cranberry, rhubarb, mustard or horseradish. Whole fish and fillets can be grilled, baked, pan-fried or braised.

Sardines

Sardines vary in
size, with the average fish about 10cm (4in) long. They have a firm, richly flavoured flesh, and are best eaten extremely fresh. They go well with citrus flavours such as lemon and orange, and with tomatoes. But they are particularly tasty when simply brushed with oil (optionally flavoured with garlic, marjoram or thyme) and then barbecued. They have a multitude of fine bones, which can sometimes be eaten but may be pulled off the meat with great care. Allow 3–5 sardines per serving. Cook whole, or fillet, and grill, barbecue or pan-fry and serve with a squeeze of lemon juice.

THE BASICS

Canned fish

A number of common canned fish make useful storecupboard standbys for when you want to make a quick meal.

Tuna

Canned in oil, brine or spring water and available as chunks or steaks, canned tuna has a different texture to fresh. It is pinkish-grey in colour, with a dry and firm texture, and the fish flakes easily. Once opened, store in the fridge and use within two days. Drain all types of tuna. Can be mixed with mayonnaise to use in sandwiches, or use in salads or add to sauces.

Sardine

Whole sardines are gutted, with their heads and tails removed, then canned in oil or tomato sauce. Canning softens the bones, making them edible. Once opened, store in the fridge for up to two days. Drain sardines in oil. Serve on toast, mash to make pâté, or add to pasta sauces.

Pilchard

These fish, which are mature sardines, are usually canned in tomato sauce. Pilchards are canned in the same way as sardines, resulting in soft, edible bones. Once opened, store in the fridge and use within two days. Serve on toast, or add to pasta sauces.

Mackerel

Skinned mackerel fillets are canned in oil, brine or a sauce such as tomato or mustard. They have a firm, meaty texture. Once opened, store in the fridge and use within two days. Drain mackerel in oil or brine. Serve on toast, or add to pasta sauces.

Salmon

Canned salmon is soft and slightly gelatinous. Although it still contains its bones, these are softened by the canning process, making them edible and a good source of calcium. Once opened, store in the fridge and use within two days. Drain and use in fishcakes, pies and sandwiches.

Vegetables
Preparing vegetables

Peeling tomatoes

1. Fill a bowl or pan with boiling water. Using a slotted spoon, add the tomato for 15–30 seconds, then remove to a board.

2. Peel off the skin; it should come away easily depending on ripeness. To remove the seeds, halve the tomato and scoop out the seeds with a spoon or cut out with a small sharp knife.

1. Cut off the stem and slit the chilli open lengthways. Using the knife, or a spoon, scrape out the seeds and the pith.

2. For diced chilli, cut into thin shreds lengthways, then cut crossways.

Seeding peppers

 Top Tip

- Chillies vary enormously in strength, from quite mild to blisteringly hot, depending on the type of chilli and its ripeness. Taste a small piece first to check it's not too hot for you.
- Be extremely careful when handling chillies not to touch or rub your eyes with your fingers, as they will sting.
- Wash knives immediately after handling chillies for the same reason. Wash hands thoroughly after handling chillies – the volatile oils will sting if accidentally rubbed into your eyes. As a precaution, use rubber gloves when preparing them, if you like.

1. Cut the pepper in half vertically and snap out the white pithy core and seeds. Trim away the rest of the white membrane with a knife.

2. Alternatively, cut off the top of the pepper, then cut away and discard the seeds and white pith.

Garlic

A head of garlic comprises many individual cloves.

1 Break off a clove from the head and put on a chopping board. Place the flat side of a large knife on top of it. Press down firmly on the flat of the blade to crush the clove and break the papery skin.

2 Cut off the base of the clove and slip the garlic out of its skin. It should come away easily.

To crush a garlic clove Put the peeled clove into a garlic press. To crush with a knife: roughly chop the peeled cloves with a pinch of salt.

To slice a garlic clove Using a rocking motion with the knife tip on the board, slice the garlic as thinly as you need.

To shred and chop Holding the slices together, shred them across the slices. Chop the shreds if you need chopped garlic.

Carrots

1 Cut off the ends. Using a vegetable peeler, peel off the skin and discard. Continue peeling the carrot into ribbon strips.

2 **Slicing** Cut slices off each of the rounded sides to make four flat surfaces that are stable on the chopping board. Hold steady with one hand and cut lengthways into even slices so they are lying in a flat stack. The stack can then be cut into batons or matchsticks.

3 **To dice carrots** turn the stack at right angles and cut through in the opposite direction.

Onions

Using a sharp knife, cut the onion in half from tip to base. Peel away all the layers of papery skin and any discoloured layers underneath.

To slice an onion Peel as above, then put one half on the board with the cut surface facing down, and slice across the onion.

To chop an onion To chop an onion, peel as above, then put the flat sides down and make three horizontal cuts from the pointed end almost to the root. Cut along its length six or seven times. Now chop across the width, from pointed end to root, to make dice. Throw away the root.

THE BASICS

51

Broccoli

1 Slice off the end of the stalk and cut 1cm (½in) below the florets. Cut the broccoli head in half.

2 Peel the thick, woody skin from the stalks and slice the stalks in half or quarters lengthways. Cut off equal-sized florets with a small knife. If the florets are very large, or if you want them for a stir-fry, you can halve them by cutting lengthways through the stalk and pulling the two halves apart.

Courgettes

Cutting diagonally is ideal for courgettes and other vegetables in a stir-fry. Wash and dry the courgette and trim the base and the stem. Trim off a piece at the base at a 45-degree angle, then repeat with the remaining courgette.

Cauliflower

First cut off the base and remove the outer leaves, then cut out the tough inner core in a cone-shaped piece. Cut off the florets in the same way as for broccoli (above). Don't cut away too much of the stalk or the florets will fall apart.

Mushrooms

Button, white, chestnut and flat mushrooms are all prepared in a similar way.

1 Wipe with a damp cloth or pastry brush to remove any dirt.

2 Button mushrooms: cut off the stalk flush with the cap base. Other mushrooms: cut a thin disc off the end of the stalk and discard. Chop or slice the mushrooms.

Leeks

As some leeks harbour a lot of grit and earth between their leaves, they need careful cleaning. Cut off the root and any tough parts. Make a cut into the leaf end of the leek, about 7.5cm (3in) deep. Hold under the cold tap while separating the cut halves to expose any grit. Wash well, then shake dry. Slice or cut into matchsticks.

Cabbage

The following method is suitable for all cabbages. The crinkly leaved Savoy cabbage may need more washing than other varieties, because its open leaves catch dirt more easily than the tightly packed white and red cabbage.

1. Pick off any of the outer leaves that are dry, tough or discoloured. Cut off the base and, using a small sharp knife, cut out as much as possible of the tough inner core in a single cone-shaped piece. Or you can cut the cabbage in half, from top to bottom, then cut out the core from each half.

2. If you need whole cabbage leaves, peel them off one by one. As you work your way down, you will need to cut out more of the core.

3. If you are cooking the cabbage in wedges, cut it in half lengthways, then cut the pieces into wedges of the required size.

Shredding cabbage
If you want fine shreds, cut the cabbage into quarters before slicing with a large cook's knife.

Potatoes

How to choose and store potatoes
Look for hard, unblemished potatoes and avoid any that are soft and wrinkled, or with green patches (which can be toxic) or shoots. New potatoes should feel slightly damp and their skins should rub off easily. If you buy potatoes in polythene bags, remove them and put them in a brown paper sack or similar, and store in a cool, dry and dark place, making sure they are not exposed to light. Maincrop potatoes keep well, but new potatoes should be used within a few days of purchase.

Preparing potatoes
Potatoes should be prepared just before you cook them, because their flesh will discolour once cut or peeled. However, you can peel potatoes and keep them covered in water up to 24 hours ahead.

Most of the nutrients in a potato are stored just beneath the skin, so where possible, cook and eat potatoes with the skin on. New potatoes can be scrubbed, or scraped with a knife. You may need to peel maincrop potatoes if you are planning to boil and mash or roast them, although they can be delicious roasted in their skins. To peel, use a sharp vegetable peeler that removes the skin in a thin, even layer.

Avocados

Prepare avocados just before serving because their flesh discolours quickly once exposed to air. Halve the avocado lengthways and twist the two halves apart. Tap the stone with a sharp knife, then twist to remove the stone. Run a knife between the flesh and skin and pull away. Slice the flesh.

Cooking vegetables

Boiling

This technique is suitable for most vegetables, but time them carefully as they can disintegrate or turn mushy if overcooked.

1 Prepare the vegetables and put them in plenty of salted cold water.

2 Cover, bring to boil, then reduce the heat and simmer until cooked. Drain in a colander.

Boiling times
Note: All timings are for peeled vegetables sliced about 2.5cm (1in) thick, except where noted.

Vegetable	Time
Beetroot (whole)	1–2 hours
Carrots	10–20 minutes
Celeriac	20–25 minutes
Corn on the cob	10–15 minutes
Green beans	4–6 minutes
Potatoes	15–20 minutes
Potatoes, new	10 minutes
Salsify	10–20 minutes
Sweet potatoes	10–15 minutes

Boiling Tips
- Don't boil very thin pieces of root vegetable – they are more likely to absorb a lot of water and disintegrate.
- Small new potatoes are the only type that takes well to boiling whole. Larger ones can start to disintegrate before they are fully cooked.

Steaming

This is a healthy cooking method, cooking the vegetables until just tender while retaining their nutrients.

1 Put the vegetables in a steamer basket set over a pan of simmering water, being careful that the water does not touch the basket.

2 Cover and cook until the vegetables are just tender.

Steaming times
Note: For soft results, add 2–3 minutes.

Vegetable	Time
Leaf spinach	1–2 minutes
Peas, beans, carrots, cabbage, cauliflower and broccoli florets	about 5 minutes
Root vegetables	5–10 minutes

Steaming Tips
- Use an uncrowded steamer so that air can circulate.
- Cut root vegetables into chunks or dice.
- Toss the vegetables now and then during steaming.
- If steaming frozen vegetables, move them around occasionally.

Microwaving

1 Cut vegetables into bite-sized pieces and put, no more than 12.5cm (5in) deep, into a microwave-proof bowl. Add a splash of water, season and cover with clingfilm. Cook at full power for 2 minutes. Toss, re-cover and cook for 2 minutes more.

2 Continue in 2-minute bursts until cooked al dente (with a little 'bite'). Toward the end of cooking, switch to 1-minute bursts.

Frying

The frying pan should have a thick base to conduct heat evenly. You can fry most things in sunflower oil, but you can also fry in butter; mushrooms taste good this way, but be careful of burning – add a little oil to avoid this.

Shallow-frying
This uses a small amount of fat – about 1cm (½in) – which is heated in the pan over a medium heat. Pieces of food should be of an even size – potato slices, for example. Don't crowd the pan – cook food in batches if necessary.

Deep-frying
This is a quick method that requires a vegetable oil to be heated in a deep pan or deep-fat fryer to a specified temperature. The pan should be no more than half-full and the oil should be brought to temperature gradually. Foods for deep-frying are often coated with batter or breadcrumbs – vegetable fritters, for example. Cook food in small quantities to avoid lowering the temperature of the oil. Never leave a pan unattended when deep-fat frying.

How to fry an onion

1 For 1 medium onion, heat 1 tbsp vegetable, sunflower or olive oil over a medium heat for 30 seconds.

2 Add the chopped onion to the pan and stir to coat in the oil for 1 minute. Turn the heat down to its lowest setting and cook for at least 15 minutes, stirring regularly to make sure the onion cooks evenly. Don't let the onion burn. Add a splash of water if it looks as if it's going to. The longer onions cook, the softer and more translucent they'll become.

THE BASICS

Cooking potatoes

Potatoes are cheap and can be cooked in lots of ways.

Boiled potatoes

Peel old potatoes, scrape new potatoes. Cut large potatoes into even-sized chunks. Put them into a pan with plenty of salted cold water. Cover, bring to the boil, then reduce the heat and simmer until cooked – about 10 minutes for new potatoes, 15–20 minutes for old.

Roast potatoes

To serve 8-10, you will need:

1.8kg (4lb) potatoes, peeled and cut into large chunks
3 tbsp vegetable oil
75g (3oz) unsalted butter
salt and ground black pepper

1   Preheat the oven to 200°C (180°C fan oven) mark 6. Put the potatoes in a pan of salted water, cover, bring to the boil and simmer for 5–6 minutes. Drain and return to the pan over a low heat. Shake until the potatoes are dry and fluffy.

2   Heat the oil and butter in a roasting tin. Put the potatoes into the tin. Toss in oil and butter and season. Add flavourings such as unpeeled garlic cloves and sprigs of rosemary, if you like. Cook in the oven for 1 hour, turning from time to time until the potatoes are brown and crisp. Adjust the seasoning and serve.

Mashed potatoes

Chips

To serve 4, you will need:
900g (2lb) potatoes such as Maris Piper
125ml (4fl oz) milk
25g (1oz) butter
salt and ground black pepper

1 Peel the potatoes and cut into even-sized chunks. Boil as above until just tender, 15–20 minutes. Test with a small knife. Drain well.

2 Put the potatoes back in the pan and cover with a clean teatowel for 5 minutes to absorb the steam, or warm them over a very low heat until the moisture has evaporated.

3 Pour the milk into a small pan and bring to the boil. Pour on to the potatoes with the butter, and season with salt and pepper.

4 Mash the potatoes until smooth, light and fluffy.

Perfect mash
Use a potato masher for perfect mash. Otherwise, use a fork, but the mash won't be lump-free. Mashing is also suitable for parsnips, sweet potatoes and celeriac.

1 Peel the potatoes and cut into chips, then dry on kitchen paper. Heat vegetable oil in a large pan or deep-fryer, if you have one, to 160°C (test by frying a small cube of bread; it should brown in 60 seconds). Fry the chips in batches for 6–7 minutes until soft. Drain on kitchen paper.

2 Turn up the heat to 190°C (a cube of bread should brown in 20 seconds). Return the chips to the pan and fry until golden brown. Drain on kitchen paper, sprinkle with salt and serve.

THE BASICS

Pasta and Noodles

Types of pasta

Penne

The name penne means 'quill', and reflects the shape of this pasta: a short hollow tube with the ends cut on the diagonal, like a quill.

To Use Cook according to the pack instructions. Serve with smooth, chunky or creamy sauces; cold in salads (drain, toss with oil, and combine when at room temperature with other salad ingredients).

Fusilli

The word fusilli means 'little spindles', and these short spirals of pasta are a popular shape.

To Use Cook according to the pack instructions. Serve with creamy sauces such as walnut, or vegetable sauces such as spinach and tomato; in salads; tossed with a sauce and baked.

Spaghetti

Taking its name from the Italian word spago, meaning 'string', spaghetti is one of the best-known and most commonly found varieties of long pasta. It consists of long, thin, round strands of pasta that vary in length and thickness. Although it is most commonly sold as plain pasta, you can also find coloured and flavoured spaghetti, including spinach and wholewheat.

To Use Cook according to the pack instructions. Serve with oil-based sauces such as garlic and olive oil, or tomato sauce.

Lasagne

These flat, rectangular sheets of pasta may be flat or rippled, with straight or ruffled edges, and are designed to be layered with sauce and baked in the oven; a classic lasagne is made with layers of meat ragu sauce and béchamel sauce, although other popular fillings include spinach and ricotta or a chunky vegetable sauce.

To Use Cook a few sheets of lasagne at a time according to the pack instructions. Layer alternately with meat or vegetable sauce and béchamel sauce, then bake. Easy-cook lasagne sheets are also available.

Ravioli

A popular and widely available type of pasta, these stuffed pasta squares with a crimped edge may be made from plain, egg or flavoured dough. Stuffings range from classics such as spinach and ricotta or minced meat, to new ideas such as crab, artichoke or pumpkin.

To Use Cook according to the pack instructions. Serve with melted butter or herb butter, or with cream or tomato sauces.

Cooking pasta

Overcooked soggy pasta is horrible to eat, so start testing it a minute before the cooking time stated on the pack. Why? Because by the time you've tasted and drained, it will be done.

Use about 1 litre (1¾ pints) of water per 100g (3½oz) of pasta. Filled pasta is the only type of pasta that needs oil in the cooking water – the oil reduces friction, which could tear the wrappers and allow the filling to come out. If the recipe calls for cooking the pasta with a sauce after it has boiled, undercook the pasta slightly when boiling it. Rinse pasta after cooking only if you are going to cool it to use in a salad, then drain well and toss with oil.

Dried pasta

1   Fill a big pan with plenty of water. Cover and bring to a boil, then once it's boiling keep the heat high so that it's constantly boiling. This will stop the pasta sticking together. Add 1 tsp salt to the water.

2   Allow 125g (4oz) pasta per person. Tip the pasta into the boiling water and stir once. If you're using spaghetti, push it into the pan and, as the ends soften, coil them round in the pan to immerse all the spaghetti in the water. Set the timer for 1 minute less than the cooking time on the pack and cook uncovered.

3   Check the pasta when the timer goes off. It should be cooked al dente: tender with a little bite at the centre. If it's done drain well. Otherwise, cook for another 30 seconds and taste again. Drain in a colander.

Fresh pasta

Fresh pasta is cooked in the same way as dried, but for a shorter time. Bring the water to the boil. Add the pasta to the boiling water all at once and stir well. Set the timer for 2 minutes and keep testing every 30 seconds until the pasta is cooked al dente: tender, but with a bite at the centre. Drain in a colander.

✅ Top Tip

Even if your mobile rings, don't be distracted from draining the pasta. If you leave it in the water for longer, it will turn soggy and can't be rescued. If you're not ready to serve the pasta right away, drain, return it to the pan and add a drizzle of oil to stop it sticking. It will be OK covered for 5–10 minutes.

THE BASICS

Noodles

Egg (wheat) noodles

These are the most versatile of Asian noodles. Like Italian pasta, they are made from wheat flour, egg and water and are available fresh or dried in various thicknesses.

1   Bring a pan of water to the boil and put the noodles in.

2   Agitate the noodles using chopsticks or a fork to separate them. This can take a minute or even more.

3   Continue boiling for 4–5 minutes until the noodles are cooked al dente: tender but with a little bite in the centre.

4   Drain well and then rinse in cold water and toss with a little oil if you are not using them immediately.

Perfect noodles
- Use 50–75g (2–3oz) uncooked noodles per person.
- Dried egg noodles are often packed in layers. As a general rule, allow one layer per person for a main dish.
- If you plan to re-cook the noodles after the initial boiling or soaking – for example, in a stir-fry – it's best to undercook them slightly.
- When cooking a layer, block or nest of noodles, use a pair of forks or chopsticks to untangle the strands from the moment they go into the water.

Glass, cellophane or bean thread noodles
These very thin noodles are made from mung beans; they need only 1 minute in boiling water.

Rice noodles
These may be very fine (rice vermicelli) or thick and flat. Most need no cooking, only soaking in warm or hot water; check the packet instructions, or cover the noodles with freshly boiled water and soak until they are al dente: tender but with a little bite at the centre. Drain well and toss with a little oil if you are not using them immediately.

Rice, Grains and Pulses

Rice

There are two main types of rice: long grain and short grain. Long-grain rice is the most often used as it is a good accompaniment. Short-grain rice is used for dishes such as risotto and paella and for puddings.

Cooking rice

Long-grain rice

1. Use 50–75g (2–3oz) raw rice per person, but measure it by volume 50–75ml (2–2½fl oz). Regular long-grain rice needs no preparation. Put the rice into a pan with a pinch of salt and twice the volume of boiling water (or stock).

2. Bring to the boil. Turn the heat down to low and set the timer for the time stated on the pack. The rice should be al dente: tender with a bite at the centre.

3. When the rice is cooked, fluff up the grains with a fork.

Thai rice

500g (1lb 2oz) Thai rice
salt
handful of mint leaves

1. Cook the rice and mint in lightly salted boiling water for 10–12 minutes until tender. Drain well and serve.

Basic pilau rice

To serve 6, you will need:
50g (2oz) butter
225g (8oz) long-grain white rice
750ml (1¼ pints) hot chicken stock (see Top Tip)
salt and ground black pepper
generous knob of butter, to serve

1 Melt the butter in a pan, add the rice and fry gently for 3–4 minutes until translucent.

2 Slowly pour in the hot stock, season, stir and cover with a tight-fitting lid. Leave, undisturbed, over a very low heat for about 15 minutes until the water has been absorbed and the rice is just tender.

3 Remove the lid and cover the surface of the rice with a clean cloth. Replace the lid and leave to stand in a warm place for about 15 minutes to dry the rice before serving.

4 Fork through and add a knob of butter to serve.

✔ Top Tip
You can use 1½ chicken stock cubes dissolved in 750ml (1¼ pints) boiling water.

Basic risotto

Italian risotto is made with medium-grain arborio, vialone nano or carnaroli rice, which release starch to give a rich, creamy texture. It is traditionally cooked on the hob, but can also be cooked in the oven by adding all the liquid in one go and cooking until the liquid is absorbed.

To serve 4, you will need:

1 onion, chopped
50g (2oz) butter
900ml (1½ pints) hot chicken stock
225g (8oz) risotto rice
50g (2oz) freshly grated Parmesan, plus extra to serve

1 Gently fry the onion in the butter for 10–15 minutes until very lightly coloured. Heat the stock in a separate pan and keep at a simmer. Add the rice to the butter and stir for 1–2 minutes until well coated.

2 Add a ladleful of stock and stir constantly until absorbed. Add the remaining stock a ladleful at a time, stirring, until the rice is al dente (tender but still with bite at the centre), 20–30 minutes (you may not need all the stock).

3 Stir in the Parmesan and serve immediately with extra cheese.

Cooking other grains

With any grain, the cooking time depends on how the grain has been processed. Bulgur wheat and barley come in several forms, so you need to check which type you have bought.

Bulgur wheat

A form of cracked wheat, bulgur is good served as an accompaniment or used in salads.

Simmering bulgur
Put in a pan with water to cover by about 2.5cm (1in). Bring to the boil, then simmer for 10–15 minutes until just tender. Drain well.

Steaming bulgur
Place the bulgur in a steamer lined with a clean teatowel and steam over boiling water for 20 minutes or until the grains are soft.

Soaking bulgur
Put the bulgur in a deep bowl. Cover with hot water and mix with a fork. Leave to steep for 20 minutes, checking to make sure there is enough water. Drain and fluff up with a fork.

Quinoa

This high-protein grain makes a good alternative to rice. Put the quinoa in a bowl of cold water. Mix well and soak for 2 minutes, Drain, then boil for 20 minutes with twice its volume of water. Remove from the heat, cover and leave to stand for 5 minutes.

Barley

There are three different types of barley: whole barley, pot barley and pearl barley. Pot and pearl are the quickest to cook and can be added to stews or served as an accompaniment. Rinse pot or pearl barley and put into a pan. Add plenty of water for pot barley and twice the volume of water to cook pearl. Bring to the boil. Turn down the heat and simmer until tender, 25–30 minutes for pearl barley and 45–50 minutes for pot.

Using beans and lentils (pulses)

Beans, pulses and lentils are the edible seeds of various leguminous plants. Rich in nutrients, they are a good source of vegetarian protein. However, it should be noted that despite being a rich source of protein, most do not constitute a whole protein (containing all eight amino acids) and need to be combined with grains or cereals to make up full protein. They are a good source of fibre, B vitamins, potassium and iron.

Many dried beans and peas need to be soaked overnight and then cooked, although lentils do not need soaking and are quicker to cook. Quicker still are canned beans: they are ready to use, but should be drained in a sieve and rinsed in cold water first.

Canned beans

Although beans and pulses are simple to cook, soaking and lengthy boiling make them impractical to cook when you don't have a lot of time at your disposal. This is why canned beans are such an invaluable storecupboard item. Most types are available ready-cooked in cans and they are relatively inexpensive, although of course they are more expensive than home-cooked beans. They tend to be very soft – certainly softer than home-cooked beans and pulses. This makes them ideal for making purées and dips. But they can also be served as an accompaniment with just brief heating, preferably with added garlic, onion or lemon juice to boost the flavour. When buying, look out for beans canned in water rather than brine, as many varieties can be high in salt.

Beans are also available to buy in microwave pouches, which are very easy to cook – follow the instructions on the packet.

To Use Drain and rinse well in cold water before using according to your recipe.

Stir-frying

Stir-fries can be as simple or as substantial as you feel like making them. They're quick to cook – but you need to have all the ingredients prepared before you start cooking. You can buy ready-prepared stir-fry vegetables, but they will be more expensive than chopping your own. Ensure your wok or pan is very hot before you start cooking and keep the ingredients moving so that they don't stick or burn.

Stir-frying is ideal for chicken and tender cuts of meat.

1 Trim off any fat, then cut the poultry or meat into even-sized strips or dice no more than 5mm (¼in) thick. Heat a wok or large pan until hot and add oil to coat the inside.

2 Add the poultry or meat and cook, stirring constantly, until just done. Remove and put to one side. Cook the other ingredients you are using for the stir-fry, then return the poultry or meat to the pan and cook for 1–2 minutes to heat through.

Which oil to use?

- Groundnut (peanut) oil has a mild flavour and is well suited to stir-frying and deep-frying as it has a high smoke point and can therefore be used at high temperatures.
- Sesame oil has a distinctive nutty flavour; it is best used in marinades or added as a seasoning to stir-fried dishes just before serving.
- Vegetable oil – which includes cold-pressed rapeseed oil, sunflower oil, or a blend of corn, soya bean, rapeseed or other oils – has a bland flavour and is suitable for stir-frying.

Stir-fried mixed vegetables

To serve 4, you will need:
450g (1lb) mixed vegetables (not starchy ones like potatoes)
1–2 tbsp vegetable oil
2 garlic cloves, peeled and crushed
2 tbsp soy sauce
2 tsp sesame oil

1 Cut the vegetables into even-sized pieces. Heat the oil in a large wok or frying pan until smoking-hot. Add the garlic and cook for a few seconds, then remove and set aside.

2 Add the vegetables to the wok, then toss and stir them. Keep them moving constantly as they cook, which will take 4–5 minutes.

3 When the vegetables are just tender, but still with a slight bite, turn off the heat. Put the garlic back into the wok and stir well. Add the soy sauce and sesame oil, toss and serve.

✓ Top Tips for Stir-frying

- Cut everything into small pieces of similar size, shape and thickness so that they cook quickly and evenly.
- If you're cooking onions or garlic with the vegetables, don't keep them over the high heat for too long or they will burn.
- Add liquids towards the end of cooking so that they don't evaporate.

THE BASICS

Herbs and Spices

Herbs

Dried herbs are excellent for adding flavour to cooked dishes, but in most cases fresh herbs have a better flavour than dried. Buy bunches of fresh herbs from the supermarket or greengrocer and store in the fridge, or buy in pots to grow on a sunny windowsill or in window boxes. All fresh herbs freeze well. Buy dried herbs in small quantities and store in an airtight container in a cool, dark place.

Using fresh herbs

Most herbs are the leaf of a flowering plant, and are usually sold with much of the stalk intact. They have to be washed, trimmed and then chopped or torn into pieces suitable for your recipe.

Washing

1   Trim the roots and part of the stalks from the herbs. Immerse in cold water and shake briskly. Leave in the water for a few minutes.

2   Lift out of the water and put in a colander or sieve, then rinse again under the cold tap. Don't pour the herbs and their water into the sieve, because dirt in the water might get caught in the leaves. Leave to drain for a few minutes, then dry thoroughly on kitchen paper or teatowels.

Chopping herbs

1. Trim the herbs by pinching off all but the smallest, most tender stalks. If the herb is one with a woody stalk, such as rosemary or thyme, it may be easier to remove the leaves by rubbing the whole bunch between your hands; the leaves should simply pull off the stems. If the herb has fleshy stalks, such as parsley or coriander, the stalks can be saved to flavour stock or soup. Tie them in a bundle with string for easy removal.

2. If you are chopping the leaves, gather them into a compact ball in one hand, keeping your fist around the ball (but being careful not to crush them).

3. Chop with a large knife, using a rocking motion and letting just a little of the ball out of your fingers at a time.

4. When the herbs are roughly chopped, continue chopping until the pieces are in small shreds or flakes

Useful herbs

Parsley

There are two types of this vivid green herb: flatleafed and curly. Parsley goes particularly well with fish, ham and vegetables and is good in stuffings for poultry, creamy sauces, and herb butters. The strongly flavoured stalks make a good addition to stocks and stews.

Mint

Mint is equally suitable for sweet and savoury dishes and there are numerous varieties each with their own subtly different flavour. It is an essential ingredient in mint sauce and jelly, tabbouleh and yogurt dips such as tzatziki and raita. Mint can also add its unmistakeable flavour to green salads and rice, as well as couscous salads and sprinkled over Indian and Thai curries, and fragrant Thai stir-fries. Its flavour also goes well with sweet dishes such as fruit salads, and it is an essential ingredient in two famous cocktails: the mojito and the mint julep. With or without alcohol, it adds a refreshing hint of flavour to summer punches and old-fashioned lemonade. Mint tea is made by infusing fresh or dried leaves in boiling water.

Bay leaf

The fresh shiny, dark green leaves of the bay laurel have a strong smell (stronger than that of the more common dried leaves), so only one or two leaves are needed per dish. Bay leaves are a popular addition to meat and tomato sauces, stews and casseroles, and can be used to flavour marinades for meat, poultry and fish. Individual leaves can be threaded between ingredients skewered on to kebabs to give some of their flavour to the meat. A bay leaf can also add a fragrant flavour to stocks and can be infused in hot milk for dishes such as béchamel sauce. To use, rinse in cold water and pat dry with kitchen paper. Pluck off one or two individual leaves. Use whole, then remove before serving.

Rosemary

A robust herb with spiky leaves and a strong, pungent flavour, rosemary is traditionally used to flavour pork or lamb and other meats such as sausages. It is also good used in hearty vegetable and bean stews and stuffings, but should always be used in moderation, as its flavour can easily become overpowering. Rosemary grows well in gardens.

Thyme

Small-leafed thyme has a strong, aromatic flavour and is extremely popular in Mediterranean cooking. Add to slowcooked stews and casseroles and cook with meat, chicken, tomatoes and Mediterranean vegetables. It also goes well with mushrooms and makes a good flavouring for strong-tasting pâtés. There are many varieties of thyme, but the most common are garden thyme and lemon thyme. The latter has a slightly subtler, more lemony flavour that goes well with fish, mild meats such as chicken, and egg dishes such as tortillas and frittatas.

Sage

Pale grey-green, velvety sage leaves have a strong, pungent flavour and it's best not to use too many of them – they add a delicious fragrance and subtlety of flavour. In Italy, sage butter is a standard accompaniment to ravioli and other stuffed pasta. It is also good drizzled over grilled white fish. To make sage butter, fry a few sage leaves in butter for a minute until crisp, then use immediately. The leaves retain their crispness and look good as well as tasting good.

Basil

This tender, fragrant herb has an intense aroma that has a natural affinity with tomatoes. Although most often associated with Italian and Mediterranean cooking, basil is also widely used in Thai cooking. Tear rather than cut basil leaves: when cut, the edges are likely to turn black. Add to cooked dishes at the last minute.

Dried spices

Many dried spices should be fried before use to remove any harshness of flavour and to enhance their taste. Whole seeds such as coriander and cumin are usually dry-fried (fried without any oil) in a heavy frying pan until they give off a rich aroma, then ground. Ground spices may be fried in oil before adding other ingredients such as vegetables or meat.

Spices tend to lose their flavour and aroma with age, so unless you use up spices very quickly, buy them in small quantities and store in an airtight container in a cool, dark place. Whole spices retain their flavour better than ground, so ideally buy whole spices such as coriander and cumin seeds and grind them as required.

Curry pastes

Indian curry pastes

In authentic Indian cooking, spices are always freshly ground and blended for each dish. The curry powders and pastes available in supermarkets tend to be generic blends of spices for the Western cook. Powders are usually described as mild, medium and hot, depending on how much chilli they contain, and would typically include key flavourings such as cumin, coriander and turmeric. There is more variety in jars of paste, but these tend to be created in terms of popular restaurant dishes such as tikka, dopiaza and jalfrezi.

Thai curry pastes

There are numerous classic paste blends used in Thai cooking, made from wet and dry spices, herbs and aromatics, but the most widely available readymade ones are red and green curry pastes. Others include yellow curry paste, orange curry paste and mussaman curry paste. Red curry paste typically includes red chillies, cumin seeds, coriander seeds, shallots, garlic, galangal, lemongrass, fresh coriander root, peppercorns and shrimp paste, although there are many variations. Green curry paste is similar to red curry paste, and would typically include green chillies and herbs.

Harissa

This spicy red chilli paste is used throughout North Africa but is particularly associated with the cooking of Tunisia and Morocco. A blend of soaked dried chillies, garlic, cumin, coriander, salt and olive oil, harissa is a lively and versatile mix that can be used in most types of savoury dish. Rose harissa is a variation made with the addition of rose petals.

Chinese five-spice powder

A combination of Sichuan peppercorns, cassia, fennel seed, star anise and cloves. This aromatic blend is widely used in Chinese stir-fries and braised dishes, and goes particularly well with duck and meat.

Garam masala

A classic combination of spices used in Indian cooking, this aromatic spice blend is usually added to dishes towards the end of cooking. Combinations and proportions of spices vary, but a typical garam masala could include coriander, cumin, cardamom and black pepper. Other popular ingredients include cinnamon, cloves and ginger.

Ras el hanout

A complex blend of fragrant dried flower petals and dried spices, ras el hanout comes from Morocco, Tunisia and Algeria. Mixtures may vary, but a typical blend might include cardamom, nutmeg, cloves, ginger and black pepper. Lavender and rose petals are also used in some recipes. Tunisian blends tend to be milder, whereas the Moroccan ones are stronger and more pungent. Ras el hanout adds a warming, spicy, fragrant taste and aroma to tagines and soups.

Quick Meals to Start the Day

Porridge with Dried Fruit

200g (7oz) rolled oats
400ml (14fl oz) milk, plus extra to
   serve
75g (3oz) mixture of chopped ready-
   to-eat dried figs, apricots and
   raisins

1   Put the oats into a large pan and add the milk and 400ml (14fl oz) water. Stir in the figs, apricots and raisins and heat gently, stirring until the porridge thickens and the oats are cooked.

2   Divide among four bowls and serve with a splash of milk.

 Timesaver Tip
If you've got a microwave oven, put the ingredients into a bowl and microwave on full power for 4–5 minutes, stirring frequently. Take out of the microwave and leave the porridge to rest for 2 minutes before serving.

QUICK MEALS TO START THE DAY

Ready in under 30 minutes
Quick and easy
Healthy and sustaining

Serves 4
Preparation time 5 minutes
Cooking time 5 minutes

Nutritional Information (Per Serving)
280 calories, 6g fat (of which 1g saturates), 49g carbohydrate, 0.2g salt
Vegetarian · Easy

Energy-boosting Muesli

1. Mix together the oats, almonds, seeds and apricots. Store in a sealable container for up to one month. Serve with milk or yogurt.

500g (1lb 2oz) porridge oats
100g (3½oz) toasted almonds, chopped (see Top Tip, page 182)
2 tbsp pumpkin seeds
2 tbsp sunflower seeds
100g (3½oz) ready-to-eat dried apricots, chopped

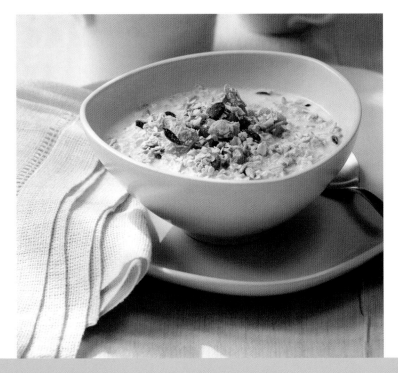

Ready in under 30 minutes
Healthy and sustaining
Make in advance

Nutritional Information (Per Serving)
208 calories, 9g fat (of which trace saturates), 28g carbohydrate, 0g salt
Vegetarian · Easy

Makes 15 servings
Preparation time 5 minutes

Apple and Almond Yogurt

500g (1lb 2oz) natural yogurt
50g (2oz) each flaked almonds
    and sultanas
2 apples

1 Put the yogurt in a bowl and add the flaked almonds and sultanas.

2 Grate the apples, add to the bowl and mix together. Chill in the fridge overnight. Use as a topping for breakfast cereal or serve as a snack.

Swap
Use pears instead of apples. Replace the sultanas with dried cranberries.

Ready in under 30 minutes
Quick and easy
Healthy choice

76

Serves 4
Preparation time 5 minutes, plus
    overnight chilling

Nutritional Information (Per Serving)
192 calories, 8g fat (of which 1g saturates), 22g carbohydrate, 0.3g salt
Vegetarian · Gluten free · Easy

Toasted Oats with Berries

1. Preheat the grill to medium. Put the hazelnuts into a bowl with the oats. Drizzle with the olive oil, mix well, then spread out on a baking sheet. Toast the oat mixture for 5–10 minutes until it starts to crisp up. Remove from the heat and set aside to cool. Store in an airtight container – it will keep for up to a week.

2. To serve, put the strawberries into a large bowl with the blueberries and yogurt. Stir in a quarter of the oats and hazelnuts, drizzle with the honey and serve immediately.

25g (1oz) hazelnuts, roughly chopped
125g (4oz) rolled oats
1 tbsp olive oil
25g (1oz) strawberries, sliced
50g (2oz) blueberries
4 tbsp Greek yogurt
½ tbsp clear honey

 Swap

Use a mixture of raspberries, blackberries or chopped nectarines or peaches instead of the strawberries and blueberries.

Ready in under 30 minutes
Healthy choice
Make in advance

QUICK MEALS TO START THE DAY

Nutritional Information (Per Serving)
327 calories, 15g fat (of which 3g saturates), 44g carbohydrate, 0.1g salt
Vegetarian · Easy

Makes 4 servings of oats, recipe serves 1
Preparation time 10 minutes, plus cooling
Cooking time 5–10 minutes

77

Apple Compôte

250g (9oz) cooking apples, peeled, cored and chopped
juice of ½ lemon
1 tbsp golden caster sugar
ground cinnamon
raisins, chopped almonds and natural yogurt to serve

1 Put the apples into a pan with the lemon juice, sugar and 2 tbsp cold water. Cook gently for 5 minutes until soft.

2 Sprinkle a little ground cinnamon over the top and chill. It will keep for up to three days.

3 Serve with the raisins, chopped almonds and yogurt.

 Timesaver Tip

If you've got a microwave oven, put the apples, lemon juice, sugar and water into a microwave-safe bowl, cover loosely with clingfilm and cook on full power in a 850W microwave for 4 minutes until the apple is just soft.

Healthy choice
Make in advance

Serves 2
Preparation time 10 minutes, plus chilling
Cooking time 5 minutes

Nutritional Information (Per Serving)
188 calories, 7g fat (of which 1g saturates), 29g carbohydrate, 0g salt
Vegetarian · Gluten free · Easy

Breakfast Bruschetta

1. Slice the banana and put into a bowl with the blueberries. Spoon in the Quark and mix well.

2. Toast the slices of bread on both sides, then spread with the blueberry mixture. Drizzle with the honey and serve immediately.

1 ripe banana
250g (9oz) blueberries
200g (7oz) Quark or cream cheese
4 slices bread
1 tbsp clear honey

Ready in under 30 minutes
Quick and easy
Five ingredients or fewer

Nutritional Information (Per Serving)
145 calories, 1g fat (of which trace saturates), 30g carbohydrate, 0.4g salt
Vegetarian · Easy

Serves 4
Preparation time 5 minutes
Cooking time 5 minutes

Cranberry and Mango Smoothie

1 ripe mango, stone removed
   (see Top Tip)
250ml (9fl oz) cranberry juice
150g (5oz) natural yogurt

1 Peel and roughly chop the mango and put into a bowl with the cranberry juice and use a stick blender to blend for 1 minute.

2 Add the yogurt and blend until smooth, then serve.

 Top Tip

To remove the stone from a mango, cut a slice down one side of the mango close to the stone in the centre. Repeat on the other side. To get the flesh out neatly, cut parallel lines into the flesh of one slice, almost to the skin. Cut another set of lines to cut the flesh into squares. Press on the skin side to turn the fruit inside out, so that the flesh is thrust outwards. Cut off the chunks as close as possible to the skin. Repeat with the other half.

Equipment Alert

You'll need a stick blender for this one.

Ready in under 30 minutes
Quick and easy
Healthy choice

Serves 2
Preparation time 5 minutes

Nutritional Information (Per Serving)
133 calories, 1g fat (of which trace saturates), 29g carbohydrate, 0.2g salt
Vegetarian · Gluten free · Easy

Summer Berry Smoothie

1. Put the bananas, yogurt and spring water into a bowl and use a stick blender to whiz until smooth. Add the frozen berries and whiz to a purée.

2. Sieve the mixture, if you like, using the back of a ladle to press it through. Pour into glasses and serve.

2 large, ripe bananas, about 450g (1lb), peeled and chopped
150g (5oz) natural yogurt
150ml (¼ pint) water
500g (1lb 2oz) frozen summer fruits

Swap
Fresh strawberries or peaches would taste great instead of the frozen summer fruits.

Equipment Alert
You'll need a stick blender for this one.

Ready in under 30 minutes
Quick and easy
Healthy choice

Nutritional Information (Per Serving)
108 calories, 1g fat (of which trace saturates), 24g carbohydrate, 0.1g salt
Vegetarian • Gluten free • Easy

Serves 6
Preparation time 10 minutes

French Toast

2 medium eggs
150ml (¼ pint) semi-skimmed milk
a generous pinch of freshly grated
    nutmeg or ground cinnamon
4 slices white bread, or fruit bread,
    crusts removed and each slice cut
    into four fingers
50g (2oz) butter
vegetable oil for frying
1 tbsp golden caster sugar

 1 Using a fork, beat the eggs, milk and nutmeg or cinnamon together in a shallow dish.

2 Dip the pieces of bread into the mixture, coating them well.

3 Heat half the butter with 1 tbsp oil in a heavy-based frying pan. When the butter is foaming, fry the egg-coated bread pieces in batches, until golden on both sides, adding more butter and oil as needed. Sprinkle with sugar to serve for brunch.

✔ Top Tips

- Use leftover bread for this tasty brunch dish.
- For a savoury version, use white bread and omit the spice and sugar; serve with tomato ketchup, or with bacon and maple syrup.

Ready in under 30 minutes
Quick and easy

Serves 4
Preparation time 5 minutes
Cooking time 10 minutes

Nutritional Information (Per Finger)
259 calories, 20g fat (of which 9g saturates), 15g carbohydrate, 0.7g salt
Vegetarian · Easy

Eggy Bread Sandwiches

1. Spread the slices of bread with a little mustard, if you like, then make a sandwich with the cheese, tomato and ham. Press down on the sandwich.

2. Beat the egg lightly in a shallow dish, then season with salt and pepper. Dip the sandwich into the egg, then turn over to coat on both sides.

3. Heat a little oil in a frying pan until hot. Fry the sandwich, pouring over any remaining egg, for 2–3 minutes on each side until golden.

2 slices bread
a little Dijon mustard (if you like)
a small piece of Cheddar cheese, grated
1 tomato, sliced
1 slice ham
1 egg
a little vegetable oil

Ready in under 30 minutes
Quick and easy

Nutritional Information (Per Serving)
515 calories, 28g fat (of which 12g saturates), 39g carbohydrate, 2.7g salt
Easy

Makes 1 sandwich
Preparation time 5 minutes
Cooking time 5–7 minutes

Quick Bacon Butty

12 bacon rashers
12 slices crusty white bread
tomato ketchup to taste

1 Heat a frying pan and fry the bacon over a medium heat until crisp. Remove from the pan and keep warm.

2 Press one side of each bread slice on the pan surface to soak up the juices. Put 2 bacon rashers on each of six slices, add ketchup, top with the remaining slices and serve.

Ready in under 30 minutes
Quick and easy
Five ingredients or fewer

Makes 6 sandwiches
Preparation time 5 minutes
Cooking time 10 minutes

Nutritional Information (Per Serving)
308 calories, 10g fat (of which 2.6g saturates), 41g carbohydrate, 3.8g salt
Easy · Dairy free

Sausage and Beans on Toast

1. Put the beans, sausage and sauce into a pan and heat gently.

2. Meanwhile, toast the bread on both sides and butter generously on one side.

3. Put two slices of toast on each plate, buttered side up, pour the sausage and beans on top and season with pepper.

415g tin baked beans
50g (2oz) sausage (chorizo is full of flavour), chopped
2 tbsp Worcestershire sauce
4 slices wholemeal bread
butter
freshly ground black pepper

Ready in under 30 minutes
Quick and easy

QUICK MEALS TO START THE DAY

Nutritional Information (Per Serving)
554 calories, 25g fat (of which 13g saturates), 66g carbohydrate, 5g salt
Easy

Serves 2
Preparation time 5 minutes
Cooking time 5–6 minutes

85

Light Bites and Quick Fixes

Garlic Bread

Posh Beans on Toast

After-the-pub Cheese on Toast

Toasted Cheese and Ham Sandwich

Snazzy Cheese on Toast

Tomato Crostini with Feta and Basil

Fancy Tuna on Toast

Sardines on Toast

Tuna Melt

Mozzarella Mushrooms on Muffins

Roast Mushrooms with Pesto

Veggie Pitta

Easy Wrap

Falafel, Rocket and Soured Cream Wrap

Throw-it-all-together Naan Pizza

Cheat's Goat's Cheese, Sausage and Courgette Pizza

Garlic Cheese Pizza

Tuna Melt Pizza

Egg and Pepper Pizza

Deli Pizza

Garlic Bread

1 large crusty loaf
175g (6oz) butter, cubed
3 garlic cloves, peeled and crushed
salt and ground black pepper

1 Preheat the grill. Cut the bread into thick slices.

2 Put the butter and garlic into a small pan and heat gently until melted. Season with salt and pepper.

3 Spoon some of the melted butter on to one side of each slice of bread. Put the slices, buttered side down, on the grill rack. Cook for 1–2 minutes until crisp and golden. Drizzle the uppermost sides with the remaining butter, turn over and cook the other side. Serve immediately.

Ready in under 30 minutes
Quick and easy

Serves 8
Preparation time 5 minutes
Cooking time 5–6 minutes

Nutritional Information (Per Serving)
400 calories, 20g fat (of which 11g saturates), 50g carbohydrate, 1.6g salt
Vegetarian · Easy

Posh Beans on Toast

1. Heat the oil in a pan over a low heat, add the garlic and cook for 1 minute, stirring gently.

2. Add the beans and chickpeas to the pan with the tomatoes and bring to the boil. Strip the leaves from the rosemary, then chop finely and add to the pan. Reduce the heat and simmer for 8–10 minutes until thickened.

3. Meanwhile, toast the bread and put on to plates. Grate the Parmesan into the bean mixture, stir once, then spoon over the bread. Serve immediately.

1 tbsp olive oil
2 garlic cloves, peeled and finely sliced
400g can borlotti or cannellini beans, drained and rinsed
400g can chickpeas, drained and rinsed
400g can chopped tomatoes
2 fresh rosemary sprigs
4 slices bread
25g (1oz) freshly grated Parmesan

Ready in under 30 minutes
Healthy choice

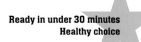

Nutritional Information (Per Serving)
364 calories, 9g fat (of which 2g saturates), 55g carbohydrate, 2.1g salt
Easy

Serves 4
Preparation time 5 minutes
Cooking time 10 minutes

After-the-pub Cheese on Toast

2 slices white or brown bread
2 tbsp mayonnaise
dash of Worcestershire sauce
125g (4oz) Cheddar or Red Leicester
    cheese, grated

1 Preheat the grill to high. Toast the bread on one side, then turn it over.

2 Spread the untoasted side of each slice with mayonnaise and sprinkle a dash of Worcestershire sauce on to each. Scatter the grated cheese over, then cook under the hot grill until golden and bubbling.

LIGHT BITES AND QUICK FIXES

Ready in under 30 minutes
Quick and easy

Serves 1
Preparation time 5 minutes
Cooking time 5 minutes

Nutritional Information (Per Serving)
895 calories, 67g fat (of which 31g saturates), 37g carbohydrate, 3.5g salt
Vegetarian • Easy

Toasted Cheese
and Ham Sandwich

1 Spread each slice of bread on both sides with the butter. Then spread one side of two slices of bread with a little mustard.

2 Divide the cheese and ham between the two mustard-spread bread slices. Put the other slice of bread on top and press down.

3 Heat a frying pan or griddle with a little butter until hot, then fry the sandwiches for 2–3 minutes on each side until golden and crispy and the cheese starts to melt.

4 Slice in half and serve immediately.

4 slices white bread
butter, softened, to spread, plus extra
    for frying
Dijon mustard, to taste
125g (4oz) cheese (Gruyère is good)
4 slices ham

Ready in under 30 minutes
Quick and easy

Nutritional Information (Per Serving)
551 calories, 35g fat (of which 22g saturates), 27g carbohydrate, 3.6g salt
Easy

Makes 2 sandwiches
Preparation time 5 minutes
Cooking time 8 minutes

Snazzy Cheese on Toast

2 thick slices bread (see Top Tip)
2 tbsp cranberry sauce
75g (3oz) blue cheese (Stilton is good)

1 Preheat the grill. Toast the bread lightly on both sides.

2 Spread one side of each with 1 tbsp cranberry sauce.

3 Crumble the cheese and sprinkle on top of the cranberry sauce.

4 Put each slice under the hot grill until the cheese melts, then eat immediately.

✓ Top Tip
Granary bread and walnut bread are really good with cheese.

Ready in under 30 minutes
Quick and easy
Five ingredients or fewer

Serves 2
Preparation time 5 minutes
Cooking time 5 minutes

Nutritional Information (Per Serving)
280 calories, 14g fat (of which 9g saturates), 27g carbohydrate, 1.4g salt
Vegetarian · Easy

Tomato Crostini
with Feta and Basil

1. Whiz the garlic, chopped basil, pinenuts, olive oil, lime zest and juice together in a blender to form a smooth paste (or chop all the ingredients and mix together). Add the feta cheese and blend until smooth, or mash. Thin with 1 tbsp water if necessary. Season with salt and pepper.

2. Put the tomatoes, tomato salsa and olives in a bow,l and gently toss them together.

3. Toast the bread. Divide the tomato mixture among the slices of toast and spoon the basil and feta mixture over the top. Garnish with basil leaves and serve.

1 small garlic clove, peeled and crushed
3 tbsp freshly chopped basil, plus extra basil leaves to garnish
25g (1oz) pinenuts
2 tbsp extra virgin olive oil
grated zest and juice of 1 lime (see Top Tip)
50g (2oz) feta cheese
4 large tomatoes, thickly sliced
150g tub fresh tomato salsa
50g (2oz) pitted black olives, roughly chopped
4 thick slices bread
salt and ground black pepper

Ready in under 30 minutes
Quick and easy
Healthy choice

 Equipment Alert

You'll need a blender for this one.

Top Tip

Zesting citrus fruit

Orange and lemon zest are important flavourings in many recipes. Most citrus fruit is sprayed with wax and fungicides or pesticides. Unless you buy unwaxed fruit, wash it with a tiny drop of washing-up liquid and warm water, then rinse with clean water and dry thoroughly on kitchen paper.

- **To use a grater**, rub the fruit over the grater, using a medium pressure to remove the zest without removing the white pith.
- **To use a zester**, press the blade into the citrus skin and run it along the surface to take off strips of zest.

LIGHT BITES AND QUICK FIXES

Nutritional Information (Per Serving)
242 calories, 17g fat (of which 3g saturates), 18g carbohydrate, 1.5g salt
Vegetarian · Easy

Serves 4
Preparation time 20 minutes
Cooking time 3 minutes

Fancy Tuna on Toast

2 x 185g cans tuna chunks in oil,
    drained and the oil kept
8 spring onions, chopped
1 yellow pepper, seeded and sliced
    (see page 50)
20 olives, pitted and halved
1 tbsp white wine vinegar
1 tsp soured cream, plus extra to serve
8 thick slices olive bread
a handful of rocket (if you like)
salt and ground black pepper

1   Put the tuna into a bowl with the spring onions, yellow pepper and olives.

2   In a separate bowl, whisk 2 tbsp of the reserved tuna oil with the vinegar and soured cream. Toss into the tuna mixture.

3   Toast the bread until golden. Divide the tuna mixture among the slices of toast, then scatter over a handful of rocket, if you like. Serve immediately, with extra soured cream in a small bowl.

 Top Tip

If you want to cut down on the fat, replace the soured cream with fat-free Greek yogurt.

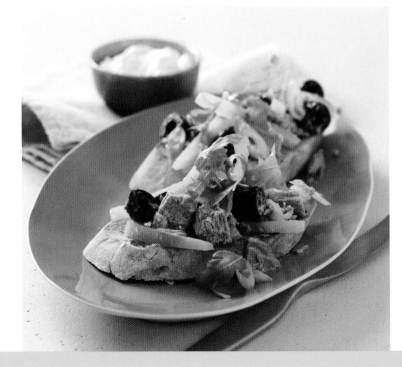

Ready in under 30 minutes
Quick and easy
Brain food

Serves 4
Preparation time 10 minutes
Cooking time 3 minutes

Nutritional Information (Per Serving)
346 calories, 14g fat (of which 2g saturates), 38g carbohydrate, 2.8g salt
Easy

Sardines on Toast

1 Preheat the grill. Toast the slices of bread on both sides.

2 Divide the tomato slices and the sardines among the toast slices, squeeze the lemon juice over them, then put back under the grill for 2–3 minutes to heat through. Scatter the parsley over the sardines, if you like, and serve immediately.

4 slices thick wholemeal bread
2 large tomatoes, sliced
2 x 120g cans sardines in olive oil, drained
juice of ½ lemon
small handful of parsley, chopped (if you like)

Ready in under 30 minutes
Quick and easy
Healthy choice

Nutritional Information (Per Serving)
240 calories, 9g fat (of which 2g saturates), 25g carbohydrate, 1.6g salt
Dairy free • Easy

Serves 4
Preparation time 5 minutes
Cooking time 8–10 minutes

Tuna Melt

2 slices bread (Granary, sourdough or
   wholemeal are good for this)
2 tomatoes, sliced
75g (3oz) canned tuna in brine,
   drained
2 tbsp mayonnaise
50g (2oz) Cheddar or Red Leicester
   cheese, grated
dash of Worcestershire sauce

1 Preheat the grill. Toast the bread on one side then turn it over.

2 Divide the sliced tomatoes between the two slices of bread, then add the tuna.

3 Spread the mayonnaise over the tuna and cover with the grated cheese. Sprinkle a dash of Worcestershire sauce on each. Grill until the cheese is golden and bubbling.

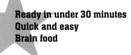 Swap

Instead of tuna use a 120g can
of sardines or mackerel.

Ready in under 30 minutes
Quick and easy
Brain food

LIGHT BITES AND QUICK FIXES

Serves 2
Preparation time 5 minutes
Cooking time 5 minutes

Nutritional Information (Per Serving)
390 calories, 21g fat (of which 8g saturates), 30g carbohydrate, 1.7g salt
Easy

Mozzarella Mushrooms
on Muffins

1 Preheat the oven to 200°C (180°C fan oven) mark 6. Lay the mushrooms side by side in a roasting tin and season with salt and pepper. Top each mushroom with a slice of red pepper and a basil leaf. Lay a slice of mozzarella on top of each mushroom. Season again. Roast in the oven for 15–20 minutes until the mushrooms are tender and the cheese has melted.

2 Meanwhile, toast the muffin halves until golden. Put a mozzarella mushroom on top of each muffin half. Serve immediately with a green salad.

8 large mushrooms
8 slices marinated red pepper
8 fresh basil leaves
150g (5oz) mozzarella, cut into
  8 slices
4 English muffins, halved
salt and ground black pepper
green salad to serve

Ready in under 30 minutes

LIGHT BITES AND QUICK FIXES

Nutritional Information (Per Serving)
137 calories, 9g fat (of which 5g saturates), 5g carbohydrate, 0.4g salt
Vegetarian • Easy

Serves 4
Preparation time 2–3 minutes
Cooking time 15–20 minutes

97

Roast Mushrooms with Pesto

8 large mushrooms
8 tbsp pesto (see Top Tip)
toasted ciabatta, salad and basil
    leaves (if you like) to serve

1 Preheat the oven to 200°C (180°C fan oven) mark 6. Put the mushrooms into an ovenproof dish, then spoon 1 tbsp pesto on top of each one.

2 Pour 150ml (¼ pint) boiling water into the dish, then cook in the oven for 15 minutes until the mushrooms are soft and the topping is hot. Serve with toasted ciabatta and salad and, if you like, scatter a few small basil leaves over the top.

 Top Tip

Pesto is a sauce made with basil, Parmesan, pinenuts, olive oil and salt and pepper. You can buy it in the supermarket. Not all pestos are vegetarian, however, so check the label.

Ready in under 30 minutes
Five ingredients or fewer
Brain food

Serves 4
Preparation time 5 minutes
Cooking time 15 minutes

Nutritional Information (Per Serving)
258 calories, 23g fat (of which 6g saturates), 1g carbohydrate, 0.5g salt
Vegetarian · Easy

Veggie Pitta

1. Split the pitta bread and spread with the hummus.

2. Fill the pitta with the cashew nuts, mushrooms, cucumber and a generous helping of fresh watercress or mixed salad leaves. Serve with extra hummus if you like, and season with pepper.

1 wholemeal pitta bread
1 tbsp hummus, plus extra to serve
15g (½ oz) unsalted cashew nuts
2 mushrooms, finely sliced
¼ cucumber, chopped
watercress or mixed salad leaves
ground black pepper

Ready in under **30 minutes**
Quick and easy
Handy for packed lunches

Nutritional Information (Per Serving)
322 calories, 11g fat (of which 2g saturates), 47g carbohydrate, 1.2g salt
Vegetarian • Easy

Makes 1
Preparation time 8 minutes

Easy Wrap

1 tsp salt
1 tsp pepper
2 cooked chicken breasts, about
    125g (4oz) each, cut into bite-size
    pieces
1 carrot, grated
1 avocado, halved, stoned, peeled
    and chopped (see page 53)
small handful of rocket
juice of 1½ lemons
3 tbsp mayonnaise
4 flour tortillas

1 Mix the salt with the pepper in a large bowl. Add the chicken, carrot, avocado and rocket, and mix well.

2 In a separate bowl, mix the lemon juice with the mayonnaise, then spread over the tortillas. Divide the chicken mixture among the tortillas, roll up and serve in napkins, if you like.

Top Tip

Quick cooking method for chicken breasts
Put the chicken on a grill rack and season with salt and pepper. Brush with oil and grill for 8–10 minutes on each side until cooked through and the juices run clear when pierced with a sharp knife.

**Ready in under 30 minutes
Five ingredients or fewer
Quick and easy**

Makes *4*
Preparation time *10 minutes*

Nutritional Information (Per Serving)
269 calories, 16g fat (of which 3g saturates), 17g carbohydrate, 1.7g salt
Dairy free • Easy

Falafel, Rocket and
Soured Cream Wrap

1 Lay the tortillas on a board and spread each one with a little soured cream.

2 Divide the rocket among the wraps and sprinkle with coriander, celery and falafel.

3 Roll up as tightly as you can, then wrap each roll in clingfilm and chill for up to 3 hours or until ready to use. To serve, unwrap and cut each roll into quarters.

6 large flour tortillas
200g (7oz) soured cream
100g (3½ oz) rocket
a small handful of fresh coriander, chopped
1 celery stick, finely chopped
180g pack ready-made falafel, roughly chopped or crumbled

Ready in under 30 minutes
Quick and easy
Handy for packed lunches

Nutritional Information (Per Serving)
270 calories, 9g fat (of which 4g saturates), 42g carbohydrate, 0.5g salt
Vegetarian • Easy

Makes 6
Preparation time 5 minutes, plus chilling

Throw-it-all-together
Naan Pizza

50g (2oz) cream cheese
1 naan bread
2 tbsp mango chutney
2 slices ham
½ yellow pepper, seeded and cut into
   strips (see page 50)
a little olive oil

1 Preheat the grill. Spread the cream cheese over the naan bread, then spoon over the mango chutney. Top with the ham and scatter the pepper strips on top.

2 Drizzle with a little olive oil and cook under the hot grill for 7–8 minutes until the pepper is tender.

Pizza Toppings

Scatter one or two of the following on top of a basic cheese and tomato pizza:

- Bits of bacon
- Rocket leaves
- Dried chilli flakes
- Capers
- Sliced sun-dried tomatoes
- Pepperoni slices
- Roasted peppers
- Sliced mushrooms

Ready in under 30 minutes
Quick and easy
Cheap eat

Serves 1
Preparation time 5 minutes
Cooking time 7–8 minutes

Nutritional Information (Per Serving)
806 calories, 39g fat (of which 17g saturates), 96g carbohydrate, 5.1g salt
Easy

Cheat's Goat's Cheese,
Sausage and Courgette Pizza

1. Put two baking sheets in the oven on separate shelves and preheat the oven to 200°C (180°F fan oven) mark 6.

2. When the baking sheets have heated up, take them out of the oven (use oven gloves) and put a pizza base on each baking sheet. Spread each one with half the mustard, then sprinkle the onion and courgette slices over the mustard. Season with salt and pepper.

3. Remove the sausages from their skins and crumble on top of each pizza with the goat's cheese. Sprinkle the thyme on top, if you like, and drizzle with the oil.

4. Put the trays back into the oven and cook for 30 minutes or until the crust and sausage are brown and the vegetables are cooked. Swap the pizzas around in the oven halfway through cooking so they cook evenly.

2 x 20.5cm (8in) pizza bases
4 tsp Dijon mustard
1 large red onion, peeled and thinly sliced
225g (8oz) courgettes, trimmed and sliced wafer thin
2 spicy pepperoni sausages
2 x 100g (3½oz) packets soft goat's cheese
fresh thyme sprigs (if you like)
olive oil to drizzle
salt and ground black pepper

£ Moneysaver Tips

- Use mozzarella instead of goat's cheese.
- Use a white onion instead of a red.

**Comfort food
Share with friends**

LIGHT BITES AND QUICK FIXES

Nutritional Information (Per Serving)
465 calories, 24g fat (of which 11g saturates), 48g carbohydrate, 2.7g salt
Easy

Makes 2 pizzas, serves 4
Preparation time 15 minutes
Cooking time 30 minutes

103

Garlic Cheese Pizza

2 x 20.5cm (8in) pizza bases
2 x 150g packs light garlic and herb
   cream cheese
12 whole sun-dried tomatoes, drained
   from oil and cut into rough pieces
40g (1½oz) pinenuts
12 fresh basil leaves (if you like)
3 tbsp olive oil

1 Put two baking sheets in the oven on separate shelves and preheat the oven to 220°C (200°F fan oven) mark 7.

2 When the baking sheets have heated up, take them out of the oven (use oven gloves) and put a pizza base on each tray. Crumble the cheese evenly over the two pizza bases and flatten with a knife, then sprinkle the sun-dried tomatoes, pinenuts and basil leaves, if you like, over the cheese. Drizzle with the oil.

3 Put the trays back into the oven and cook for 30 minutes or until pale golden and cooked to the centre. Swap the pizzas around in the oven halfway through cooking so that they cook evenly.

£ Moneysaver Tip
Instead of pinenuts use chopped
unsalted cashew nuts or peanuts.

Comfort food
Share with friends

Makes 2 pizzas, serves 4
Preparation time 15 minutes
Cooking time 30 minutes

Nutritional Information (Per Serving)
658 calories, 46g fat (of which 12g saturates), 48g carbohydrate, 1.9g salt
Easy

Tuna Melt Pizza

1   Put two baking sheets in the oven on separate shelves and preheat the oven to 220°C (200°C fan oven) mark 7.

2   When the baking sheets have heated up, take them out of the oven (use oven gloves) and put a pizza base on each tray. Spread each pizza base with 2 tbsp sun-dried tomato pesto. Top each with half the tuna, half the anchovies and half the grated cheese. Put back into the oven and cook for 10–12 minutes until the cheese has melted. Sprinkle with rocket to serve, if you like.

2 large pizza bases
4 tbsp sun-dried tomato pesto
2 x 185g cans tuna, drained
50g can anchovies, drained and chopped
125g (4oz) mature Cheddar cheese, grated
rocket to serve (if you like)

£ Moneysaver Tip
Instead of sun-dried tomato pesto use basil pesto.

Try Something Different
Ham and pineapple
Spread the pizza bases with 4 tbsp tomato pasta sauce. Top with a 225g can drained unsweetened pineapple chunks, 125g (4oz) diced ham and 125g (4oz) grated Gruyère cheese.

Brain food
Comfort food
Share with friends

LIGHT BITES AND QUICK FIXES

Nutritional Information (Per Serving)
688 calories, 26g fat (of which 9g saturates), 72g carbohydrate, 3.5g salt
Easy

Serves 4
Preparation time 5 minutes
Cooking time 10–12 minutes

105

Egg and Pepper Pizza

150g (5oz) red and yellow marinated
    peppers in oil
8 tbsp passata sauce (puréed and
    sieved tomatoes, available in jars)
4 small pizza bases
4 medium eggs
125g (4oz) watercress, washed and
    stalks removed

1. Put two large baking sheets, big enough to hold two pizzas each, into the oven and preheat the oven to 220°C (200°C fan oven) mark 7.

2. Drain the peppers but keep the oil. Chop the peppers into thin strips. When the baking sheets have heated up, take them out of the oven (use oven gloves) and put two pizza bases on each tray. Spoon 2 tbsp passata over each pizza base and scatter strips of pepper around the edges. Make a dip in the passata in the middle of each pizza and break an egg into it. Put in the oven and cook for 12 minutes until the egg is thoroughly cooked.

3. Top the pizzas with the watercress, drizzle with a little of the reserved oil from the peppers and serve.

£ **Moneysaver Tip**

Instead of passata, spread the
bases with tomato purée.

Five ingredients or fewer
Share with friends
Great for parties

Serves 4
Preparation time 15 minutes
Cooking time 12 minutes

Nutritional Information (Per Serving)
403 calories, 13g fat (of which 2g saturates), 61g carbohydrate, 1g salt
Vegetarian · Gluten free · Easy

Deli Pizza

1 Put a large baking sheet on the top shelf of the oven and preheat the oven to 220°C (200°C fan oven) mark 7.

2 Spread a thin layer of the tomato sauce over each of the pizza bases, leaving a 2.5cm (1in) border around the edge. Top with dollops of goat's cheese, then scatter over the red onion, tomatoes and olives.

3 Slide one of the pizzas on to the hot baking sheet and bake for 15 minutes or until golden and crisp. Repeat with the second pizza base. Scatter the torn basil over and serve with salad.

6 tbsp tomato pizza sauce
2 large pizza bases
100g (3½ oz) soft goat's cheese
1 red onion, peeled and finely sliced
100g (3½ oz) sunblush tomatoes
100g (3½ oz) olives
a handful of fresh basil, roughly torn
green salad to serve

 Swap

Try marinated peppers, artichokes or chargrilled aubergines instead of the olives and sunblush tomatoes.

Ready in under 30 minutes
Quick and easy
Share with friends

Nutritional Information (Per Serving)
440 calories, 15g fat (of which 5g saturates), 64g carbohydrate, 2.8g salt
Vegetarian • Easy

Serves 4
Preparation time 5 minutes
Cooking time 15 minutes

Salads

Mixed Leaf Salad

3 round lettuce hearts, roughly
   shredded
100g (3½ oz) watercress
2 ripe avocados, halved, stoned,
   peeled and roughly chopped (see
   page 53)
1 box salad cress, chopped
100g (3½ oz) sugarsnap peas,
   roughly sliced
4 tbsp French Dressing (see page 30)

1 Put the lettuce hearts into a bowl and add the watercress, avocados, salad cress and sugarsnap peas. Pour the dressing over the salad and toss to mix; serve immediately.

Ready in under 30 minutes
Quick and easy
Healthy choice

Serves 8
Preparation time 10 minutes

Nutritional Information (Per Serving)
112 calories, 11g fat (of which 2g saturates), 2g carbohydrate, 0.1g salt
Vegetarian · Dairy free · Gluten free · Easy

Simple Tomato Salad

1 Slice the tomatoes and arrange on a plate. Sprinkle with a pinch of sugar and season with salt and pepper. Leave for 20 minutes to allow the seasonings to draw out the juices.

2 Drizzle with the oil and serve with toasted bread.

8 medium-size tomatoes
golden caster sugar
1 tbsp extra virgin olive oil
salt and ground black pepper
toasted bread to serve

Ready in under 30 minutes
Quick and easy
Healthy choice

SALADS

Nutritional Information (Per Serving)
39 calories, 2g fat (of which trace saturates), 4g carbohydrate, 0.6g salt
Vegetarian · Dairy free · Easy

Serves 6
Preparation time 15 minutes

Upmarket Potato Salad

550g (1¼lb) new potatoes
6 tbsp mayonnaise
2 tbsp crème fraîche
2 tbsp white wine vinegar
2 shallots, finely chopped
4 tbsp chopped gherkins (if you like)
2 tbsp olive oil
salt and ground black pepper

1 Cook the potatoes in a pan of lightly salted boiling water for 15–20 minutes until tender. Drain, leave to cool slightly, then chop.

2 Mix together the mayonnaise, crème fraîche, vinegar, shallots, gherkins, if you like, and oil. Season with salt and pepper, and mix with the potatoes. Leave to cool, then chill until ready to serve.

£ Moneysaver Tips

- Use spring onions instead of shallots.
- Use 8 tbsp mayonnaise instead of crème fraîche.

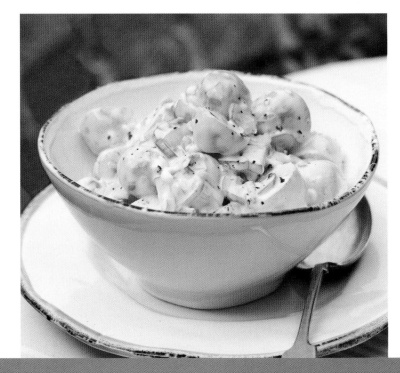

Comfort food
Share with friends
Make in advance

SALADS

112

Serves 4
Preparation time 10 minutes
Cooking time 15–20 minutes

Nutritional Information (Per Serving)
335 calories, 26g fat (of which 6g saturates), 24g carbohydrate, 0.3g salt
Vegetarian • Gluten free • Easy

Easy Bulgur Wheat Salad

1 Cook the bulgur wheat according to the pack instructions. Leave to cool slightly.

2 Stir in the herbs, lemon juice and nuts, and season with salt and pepper. Serve.

200g (7oz) bulgur wheat
(see page 64 and Timesaver Tip)
3 tbsp each freshly chopped mint
and parsley
juice of 1 lemon
1 tbsp roughly chopped pistachio nuts
salt and ground black pepper

Timesaver Tip
Use couscous instead of bulgur wheat. Soak it in boiling water for 5–10 minutes.

Ready in under 30 minutes
Quick and easy
Healthy and sustaining

SALADS

Nutritional Information (Per Serving)
399 calories, 6g fat (of which 1g saturates), 77g carbohydrate, 0.7g salt
Vegetarian • Dairy free • Easy

Serves 2
Preparation time 10 minutes
Cooking time 10 minutes

Easy Coleslaw

¼ each medium red and white
    cabbage, shredded
1 carrot, grated
20g (¾oz) flat-leafed parsley,
    finely chopped

FOR THE DRESSING
1½ tbsp red wine vinegar
4 tbsp olive oil
½ tsp Dijon mustard
salt and ground black pepper

 To make the dressing, put the vinegar into a small bowl, add the olive oil and mustard, season well with salt and pepper and mix well.

 Put the cabbage and carrot into a large bowl and toss to mix well. Add the parsley.

3 Mix the dressing again, pour over the cabbage mixture and toss well to coat.

£ Moneysaver Tips
- Instead of red cabbage, use all white cabbage.
- Any mustard can be used instead of the Dijon, but if using English mustard you will need only ½ tsp, as it's stronger.

⭐ **Ready in under 30 minutes**
Quick and easy
Healthy choice

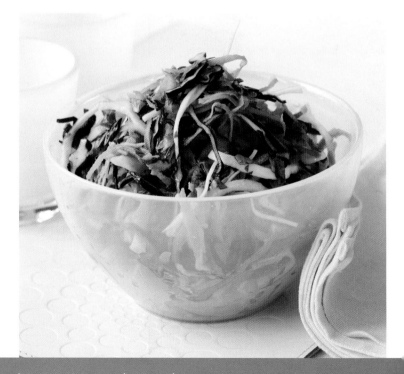

SALADS

Serves 6
Preparation time 15 minutes

Nutritional Information (Per Serving)
92 calories, 8g fat (of which 1g saturates), 5g carbohydrate, 0.1g salt
Vegetarian · Gluten free · Dairy free · Easy

Herring and Potato Salad

1. Put the potatoes into a pan of cold water, bring to the boil and cook for 15–20 minutes until tender. Drain, then cut in half.

2. Meanwhile, make the dressing. Mix the soured cream, mayonnaise and dill together in a large bowl. Season well with salt and pepper.

3. Put the potatoes, gherkins and herrings into a bowl with the dressing and toss together. Check the seasoning and serve.

1kg (2¼ lb) new potatoes, scrubbed
8 gherkins, thinly sliced
2 x 280g tubs sweet cured herrings, drained and sliced into 2cm (¾ in) strips

FOR THE SOURED CREAM DRESSING
2 tbsp soured cream
6 tbsp mayonnaise
2 tbsp freshly chopped dill
salt and ground black pepper

£ Moneysaver Tip
Instead of soured cream, increase the amount of mayonnaise to 8 tbsp.

Brain food
Share with friends

SALADS

Nutritional Information (Per Serving)
610 calories, 33g fat (of which 4g saturates), 54g carbohydrate, 2.9g salt
Gluten free · Easy

Serves 4
Preparation time 15 minutes
Cooking time 15–20 minutes

Easy Tuna Salad

400g can mixed beans, drained and
   rinsed
125g (4oz) tuna, flaked
½ cucumber, chopped
1 red onion, peeled and finely sliced
2 ripe tomatoes, chopped
2 celery sticks, chopped
handful of baby spinach leaves
1 tbsp olive oil
2 tsp red wine vinegar
salt and ground black pepper

1 Put the beans into a bowl and add the tuna, cucumber, red onion, tomatoes, celery and spinach.

2 Mix together the oil and vinegar, season with salt and pepper, then toss through the bean mix and serve.

 Moneysaver Tip

Instead of spinach leaves, use lettuce or salad leaves.

 Top Tip

If you want to make this salad for a packed lunch, add the cucumber and leaves at the last minute. They won't be as crisp when you eat them as when the salad is freshly made but it will still taste good.

Ready in under 30 minutes
Quick and easy
Cheap eat

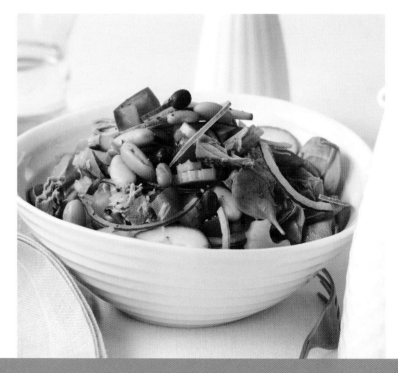

SALADS

116

Serves 2
Preparation time 10 minutes

Nutritional Information (Per Serving)
313 calories, 8g fat (of which 1g saturates), 35g carbohydrate, 2.1g salt
Gluten free · Dairy free · Easy

Tuna, Bean
and Red Onion Salad

1. Put the beans, onion slices and vinegar into a bowl, season with a little salt and mix well. Add the tuna with its oil, breaking the fish into large flakes.

2. Add half the chopped parsley and season generously with pepper. Toss the salad, then scatter the remaining parsley over the top. Serve with a green salad and plenty of warm crusty bread.

400g can cannellini beans, drained and rinsed
1 small red onion, peeled and very finely sliced
1 tbsp red wine vinegar
225g can tuna steak in oil
2 tbsp freshly chopped parsley
salt and ground black pepper

Ready in under 30 minutes
Quick and easy
Healthy and sustaining

SALADS

Nutritional Information (Per Serving)
190 calories, 6g fat (of which 1g saturates), 15g carbohydrate, 1.1g salt
Vegetarian · Gluten free · Dairy free · Easy

Serves 4
Preparation time 5 minutes

Greek Pasta Salad

3 tbsp olive oil
2 tbsp lemon juice
150g (5oz) cooked pasta shapes
   (see page 59), cooled
75g (3oz) feta cheese, crumbled
3 tomatoes, roughly chopped
2 tbsp small pitted black olives
½ cucumber, roughly chopped
1 small red onion, peeled and finely
   sliced
salt and ground black pepper
freshly chopped mint and lemon zest
   (see Top Tip, page 93) to garnish
   (if you like)

 1 Mix the oil and lemon juice together in a bowl, then add the pasta, feta cheese, tomatoes, olives, cucumber and onion.

2 Season with salt and pepper and stir to mix, then garnish with chopped mint and lemon zest, if you like, and serve.

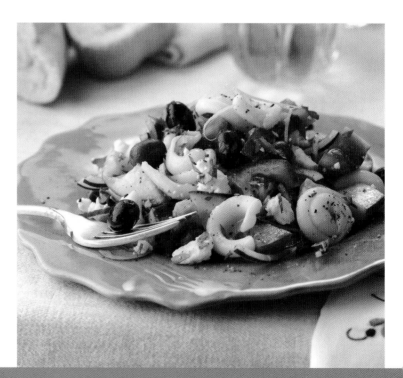

Healthy choice
Quick and easy
Handy for packed lunches

SALADS

Serves 2
Preparation time 10 minutes
Cooking time 10–15 minutes

Nutritional Information (Per Serving)
382 calories, 27g fat (of which 8g saturates), 25g carbohydrate, 2.5g salt
Vegetarian · Easy

Pasta and Avocado Salad

1. Mix together the mayonnaise, pesto and avocados, then mix with the pasta. If the dressing is too thick, dilute with a little water (use the pasta cooking water if you have it).

2. Decorate with basil leaves, if you like, and serve.

2 tbsp mayonnaise
2 tbsp pesto (see Top Tip, page 98)
2 ripe avocados, halved, stoned, peeled and cut into cubes (see page 53)
225g (8oz) cooked pasta shapes (see page 59), cooled
a few basil leaves (if you like)

Top Tip
If you have any leftover pasta from an evening meal it's always worth saving it to make a pasta salad the next day.

Ready in under **30 minutes**
Quick and easy
Healthy and sustaining

SALADS

Nutritional Information (Per Serving)
626 calories, 52g fat (of which 10g saturates), 28g carbohydrate, 1.2g salt
Vegetarian • Dairy free • Easy

Serves 2
Preparation time 5 minutes

Pasta, Salami and Tapenade Salad

3 x 225g tubs pasta salad in tomato
    sauce
75g (3oz) pepper salami, shredded
3 tbsp black olive tapenade
3 tbsp freshly chopped chives
salt and ground black pepper

1 Turn the pasta salad into a large bowl and add the salami, tapenade and chives. Toss everything together and season with pepper. Check for seasoning before adding salt – the tapenade may have made the salad salty enough.

2 Pile the salad into a large bowl. If not being served straight away, this salad is best kept in a cool place (but not chilled) until needed.

Moneysaver Tip
Instead of chives, use spring onions.

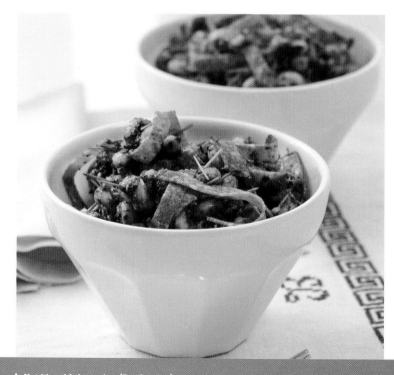

★ **Ready in under 30 minutes**
Quick and easy
Five ingredients or fewer

SALADS

Serves 4
Preparation time 5 minutes

Nutritional Information (Per Serving)
332 calories, 20g fat (of which 6g saturates), 28g carbohydrate, 2g salt
Dairy free · Easy

Red Pepper Pasta Salad

1 Mix the oil with the garlic, mustard and vinegar in a small bowl. Stir into the cooked pasta and leave to cool.

2 Season with salt and pepper, add the sliced peppers and serve sprinkled with the herbs, if you like.

6 tbsp olive oil
1 garlic clove, crushed
2 tsp Dijon mustard
2 tbsp balsamic vinegar
350g (12oz) freshly cooked pasta shapes (see page 59), drained
2 roasted red peppers, peeled, seeded and sliced
3 tbsp freshly chopped herbs, such as parsley, thyme or basil (if you like)
salt and ground black pepper

Healthy choice
Handy for packed lunches
Cheap eat

SALADS

Nutritional Information (Per Serving)
275 calories, 18g fat (of which 3g saturates), 26g carbohydrate, 0.2g salt
Vegetarian · Dairy free · Easy

Serves 4
Preparation time 10 minutes, plus cooling   **121**

Simple Bean Salad

2 tbsp olive oil, plus extra to drizzle
2 garlic cloves, peeled and sliced
2 x 400g cans flageolet beans,
    drained and rinsed
2 tbsp pesto (see Top Tip, page 98)
lemon juice to taste
a small handful of basil leaves (if you
    like)
salt and ground black pepper

1 Put the oil into a small pan and fry the garlic until golden. Stir in the flageolet beans, then take off the heat and leave to marinate in the oil for 10–15 minutes.

2 When ready to serve, drizzle a little oil over the beans until generously coated. Add the pesto and lemon juice to taste and season with salt and pepper, then stir in the basil leaves, if you like.

Swap
Instead of flageolet beans, use cannellini, haricot or borlotti beans.

Ready in under 30 minutes
Healthy choice
Handy for packed lunches

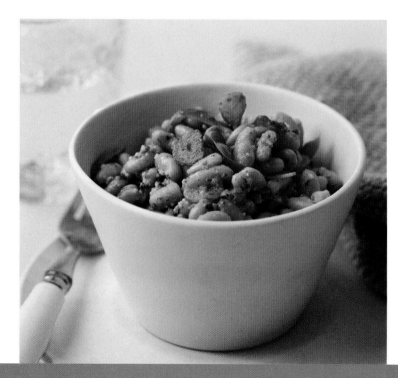

Serves 6
Preparation time 5 minutes, plus
    10–15 minutes marinating
Cooking time 5 minutes

Nutritional Information (Per Serving)
208 calories, 10g fat (of which 2g saturates), 21g carbohydrate, 1.2g salt
Vegetarian · Gluten free · Easy

Bean and Chorizo Salad

 1 Put the borlotti beans into a large bowl and add the celery, chorizo, shallots and parsley.

2 To make the dressing, whisk together the lemon zest, lemon juice and olive oil in a small bowl. Season with salt and pepper and whisk again to combine.

3 Pour the dressing over the bean mixture, toss together and serve.

400g can borlotti beans, drained and rinsed
4 large celery sticks, finely sliced
75g (3oz) chorizo sausage, diced
2 shallots, peeled and finely chopped
2 tbsp freshly chopped flat-leafed parsley
grated zest of ½ lemon (see Top Tip, page 93) plus 1 tbsp lemon juice
4 tbsp extra virgin olive oil
salt and ground black pepper

 Swap
- Instead of shallots use 1 small onion.
- Use mixed beans or flageolet beans instead of borlotti beans.

Ready in under 30 minutes
Healthy choice
Cheap eat

SALADS

Nutritional Information (Per Serving)
295 calories, 19g fat (of which 4g saturates), 20g carbohydrate, 1.9g salt
Dairy free · Easy

Serves 4
Preparation time 15 minutes

123

Bacon and Egg Salad

4 medium eggs
250g (9oz) rindless smoked bacon
   rashers
150g (5oz) cherry tomatoes
2 thick slices bread, with crusts
   removed
2 tbsp mayonnaise
juice of ½ lemon
25g (1oz) Parmesan, freshly grated
2 Little Gem lettuces
ground black pepper

1 Heat a pan of water until simmering, add the eggs and boil for 6 minutes. Cool completely under cold water, peel and set aside.

2 Meanwhile, heat a frying pan, then fry the bacon for 5 minutes until crisp. Remove from the pan, chop into large pieces and leave to cool.

3 Add the tomatoes and bread to the pan and fry for 2–3 minutes until the bread is crisp and the tomatoes are starting to char. Remove from the heat, chop the bread into bite-size pieces and put to one side.

4 To make the dressing, put the mayonnaise into a bowl and squeeze in the lemon juice. Add the Parmesan, mix, then season with pepper.

5 Separate the lettuce leaves and put into a large bowl. Add the bacon, tomatoes and bread, toss lightly, then divide among four plates. Cut the eggs in half and add one egg to each plate. Drizzle the dressing over.

Ready in under 30 minutes
Quick and easy
Cheap eat

SALADS

Serves 4
Preparation time 10 minutes
Cooking time 10 minutes

Nutritional Information (Per Serving)
360 calories, 27g fat (of which 8g saturates), 9g carbohydrate, 3.1g salt
Easy

Easy Chicken Salad

1. Put the chicken into a shallow bowl. Add the carrot, celery, cucumber and cherry tomatoes.

2. Top with the hummus and serve with lemon for squeezing over the salad.

100g (3½ oz) shredded roast chicken, skin discarded
1 carrot, chopped
1 celery stick, chopped
¼ cucumber, chopped
handful of ripe cherry tomatoes, chopped
1 tbsp hummus
¼ lemon to serve

Try Something Different

- Add a few pumpkin seeds or sunflower seeds, or a handful of sprouted seeds such as alfalfa, or chopped watercress.
- For extra bite, add a little finely chopped red chilli; for extra sweetness, add some strips of red pepper; for extra flavour, add some chopped coriander or torn basil leaves.

Ready in under 30 minutes
Quick and easy
Healthy choice

SALADS

Nutritional Information (Per Serving)
323 calories, 18g fat (of which 5g saturates), 17g carbohydrate, 0.9g salt
Gluten free · Dairy free · Easy

Serves 1
Preparation time 10 minutes

125

Stir-fries

Bean Sprouts with Peppers and Chillies
Mushrooms with Cashew Nuts
Stir-fried Courgettes, Mangetouts and Peas
Stir-fried Veg with Crispy Crumbs
Sweet Chilli Tofu Stir-fry
Chickpea and Chilli Stir-fry
Rice and Red Pepper Stir-fry
Five-minute Stir-fry
Stir-fried Salmon and Broccoli
Chicken Stir-fry with Noodles

Bean Sprouts with Peppers and Chillies

3 tbsp vegetable oil

2 garlic cloves, peeled and chopped

2.5cm (1in) piece fresh root ginger, peeled and chopped

6 spring onions, cut into 2.5cm (1in) pieces

1 red pepper, seeded and thinly sliced

1 yellow pepper, seeded and thinly sliced

2 green chillies, seeded and finely chopped (see page 50)

350g (12oz) bean sprouts

1 tbsp dark soy sauce

1 tbsp sugar

1 tbsp malt vinegar

a few drops of sesame oil (if you like)

boiled rice (see page 61) with 2 tbsp freshly chopped coriander stirred through (if you like), to serve

1 Heat the oil in a wok or large frying pan. Add the garlic, ginger, spring onions, peppers, chillies and bean sprouts and stir-fry over a medium heat for 3 minutes.

2 Add the soy sauce, sugar and vinegar and fry, stirring, for a further 1 minute.

3 Sprinkle with a few drops of sesame oil, if you like, then serve immediately with coriander rice.

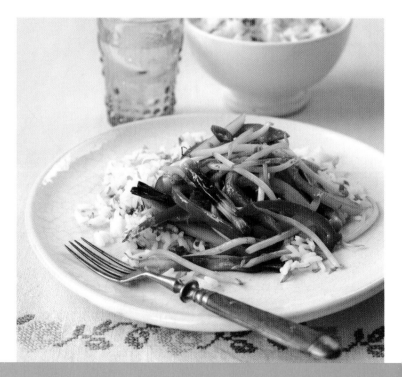

Ready in under 30 minutes
Quick and easy
Healthy choice
Cheap eat

STIR-FRIES

128

Serves 4

Preparation time 10 minutes

Cooking time 4 minutes

Nutritional Information (Per Serving)

149 calories, 9g fat (of which 1g saturates), 14g carbohydrate, 0.7g salt

Vegetarian · Dairy free

Mushrooms
with Cashew Nuts

1 Heat the oil in a wok or large frying pan. Add the nuts and cook over a high heat for 2–3 minutes until golden. Add the mushrooms and cook for a further 2–3 minutes until tender, stirring frequently.

2 Stir in the lemon juice and coriander and season to taste with salt and pepper. Heat until bubbling. Remove the pan from the heat and stir in the cream, if you like. Adjust the seasoning if necessary and serve garnished with coriander sprigs, if you like.

1 tbsp vegetable oil
25g (1oz) unsalted cashew nuts
225g (8oz) mushrooms, sliced
1 tbsp lemon juice
4 tbsp freshly chopped coriander, plus fresh sprigs to garnish (if you like)
1 tbsp single cream (if you like)
salt and ground black pepper

Ready in under 30 minutes
Quick and easy
Five ingredients or fewer
Cheap eat

STIR-FRIES

Nutritional Information (Per Serving)
75 calories, 6g fat (of which 1g saturates), 2g carbohydrate, 0.1g salt
Vegetarian · Gluten free · Easy

Serves 4
Preparation time 5 minutes
Cooking time 5–8 minutes

129

Stir-fried Courgettes,
Mangetouts and Peas

2 tbsp vegetable oil
225g (8oz) courgettes, trimmed and
    thinly sliced (see page 52)
175g (6oz) mangetouts
25g (1oz) butter
175g (6oz) frozen peas, thawed
salt and ground black pepper

1 Heat the oil in a wok or large frying pan, add the courgettes and stir-fry for 1–2 minutes. Add the mangetouts and cook for 1 minute.

2 Add the butter and peas and cook for 1 minute. Season to taste with salt and pepper and serve immediately.

 Swap
Try other vegetables, such as thinly sliced leeks, broccoli florets, spring onions or pak choi.

Ready in under 30 minutes
Quick and easy
Healthy choice
Five ingredients or fewer

Serves 6
Preparation time 5 minutes
Cooking time 3–4 minutes

Nutritional Information (Per Serving)
100 calories, 8g fat (of which 3g saturates), 5g carbohydrate, 0.1g salt
Vegetarian · Gluten free · Easy

Stir-fried Veg
with Crispy Crumbs

1 If you have one, whiz the bread in a food processor to make breadcrumbs. Otherwise, cut it into strips with a bread knife, then cut the bread up into crumbs, or use a grater (but watch your fingers). Heat 1 tbsp oil in a large, non-stick frying pan or wok. Add the breadcrumbs and stir-fry for 4–5 minutes until crisp. Remove from the pan and set aside on a piece of kitchen paper.

2 Heat the remaining oil in the frying pan until hot. Add the broccoli, carrot and pepper and stir-fry over a high heat for 4–5 minutes until they're starting to soften. Add the anchovies, if you like, and continue to cook for a further 5 minutes until slightly softened. Serve the vegetables immediately, scattered with the breadcrumbs.

1 thick slice wholemeal bread, crusts removed
2 tbsp olive oil
1 broccoli head, chopped into florets (see page 52)
1 large carrot, cut into thin strips (see page 52)
1 red pepper, seeded and cut into thin strips (see page 50)
4 anchovy fillets, chopped (if you like)

 Swap
Try 400g (14oz) cauliflower florets instead of the broccoli.

Healthy choice
Cheap eat
Brain food
Share with friends

STIR-FRIES

Nutritional Information (Per Serving)
145 calories, 8g fat (of which 1g saturates), 13g carbohydrate, 0.5g salt
Dairy free · Easy

Serves 4
Preparation time 10 minutes
Cooking time 15–20 minutes

131

Sweet Chilli Tofu Stir-fry

200g (7oz) firm tofu
4 tbsp sweet chilli sauce
2 tbsp light soy sauce
1 tbsp sesame seeds
2 tbsp toasted sesame oil
600g (1lb 5oz) ready-prepared mixed
   stir-fry vegetables, such as carrots,
   broccoli, mangetouts and bean
   sprouts
a handful of pea shoots or young
   salad leaves to garnish (if you like)
boiled rice to serve (see page 61)

1 Drain the tofu, pat it dry and cut it into large cubes. Put the tofu into a shallow container and pour 1 tbsp sweet chilli sauce and 1 tbsp light soy sauce over it. Cover and marinate for 10 minutes.

2 Meanwhile, toast the sesame seeds in a hot wok or large frying pan until golden. Tip on to a plate.

3 Return the wok or frying pan to the heat and add 1 tbsp sesame oil. Add the marinated tofu and stir-fry for 5 minutes until golden. Remove and set aside.

4 Heat the remaining 1 tbsp oil in the pan, add the vegetables and stir-fry for 3–4 minutes until just tender. Stir in the cooked tofu.

5 Pour the remaining sweet chilli sauce and soy sauce into the pan, toss well and cook for a further minute until heated through. Sprinkle with the toasted sesame seeds and pea shoots or salad leaves, if you like, and serve immediately, with rice.

Healthy choice

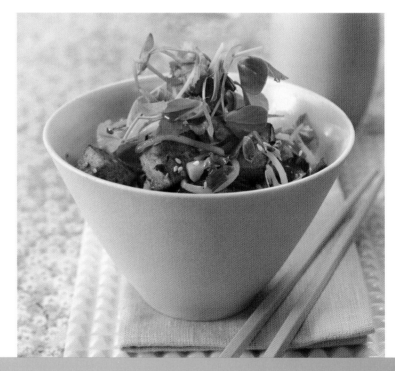

Serves 4
Preparation time 5 minutes, plus marinating
Cooking time 12 minutes

Nutritional Information (Per Serving)
167 calories, 11g fat (of which 2g saturates), 5g carbohydrate, 1.6g salt
Vegetarian · Dairy free · Easy

Chickpea and Chilli Stir-fry

1 Heat the oil in a wok or large frying pan. Add the cumin and fry for 1–2 minutes. Add the onion and stir-fry for 5–7 minutes.

2 Add the garlic and chilli and stir-fry for 2 minutes.

3 Add the chickpeas to the wok with the tomatoes. Reduce the heat and simmer until the chickpeas are hot. Season with salt and pepper. Add the spinach and cook for 1–2 minutes until the leaves have wilted. Serve with brown rice or pasta.

2 tbsp olive oil
1 tsp ground cumin
1 red onion, peeled and sliced
2 garlic cloves, peeled and finely chopped
1 red chilli, seeded and finely chopped (see page 50)
2 × 400g cans chickpeas, drained and rinsed
400g (14oz) cherry tomatoes
125g (4oz) baby spinach leaves
brown rice or pasta to serve (see pages 61 and 59)

£ Moneysaver Tips

- Instead of red onion, use white.
- Use sliced spinach instead of the baby leaves.

STIR-FRIES

Nutritional Information (Per Serving)
258 calories, 11g fat (of which 1g saturates), 30g carbohydrate, 1g salt
Vegetarian · Dairy free · Easy

Serves 4
Preparation time 10 minutes
Cooking time 15–20 minutes

Rice and Red Pepper Stir-fry

75g (3oz) long-grain rice
200ml (7fl oz) hot vegetable stock
    (see Top Tip)
2 tsp vegetable oil
½ onion, peeled and thinly sliced
2 streaky bacon rashers, chopped
1 small red pepper, seeded and cut
    into chunks (see page 50)
a handful of frozen peas
a dash of Worcestershire sauce

1 Put the rice into a pan and pour in the hot stock. Cover the pan and bring to the boil, then reduce the heat and simmer for 10 minutes or until the rice is tender and the liquid has been absorbed.

2 Meanwhile, heat the oil in a wok or large frying pan over a medium heat. Add the onion and fry for 5 minutes. Add the bacon and pepper and fry for a further 5 minutes or until the bacon is crisp.

3 Stir the cooked rice and the peas into the onion mixture and cook, stirring occasionally, for 2–3 minutes until the rice and peas are hot. Add a dash of Worcestershire sauce and serve.

 Top Tip
You can use ½ vegetable stock cube dissolved in 200ml (7fl oz) boiling water.

Ready in under 30 minutes
Quick and easy
Healthy and sustaining
Comfort food

STIR-FRIES

Serves 4
Preparation time 5 minutes
Cooking time 15 minutes

Nutritional Information (Per Serving)
157 calories, 5g fat (of which 1g saturates), 22g carbohydrate, 0.5g salt
Gluten free · Dairy free · Easy

Five-minute Stir-fry

1. Heat the oil in a large wok or frying pan, add the prawns and sweet chilli and ginger sauce and stir-fry for 2 minutes.

2. Add the mixed vegetables and stir-fry for a further 2–3 minutes until the prawns are cooked and the vegetables are heated through. Serve immediately.

1 tbsp sesame oil
175g (6oz) raw peeled prawns, deveined (see Swap)
50ml (2fl oz) ready-made sweet chilli and ginger sauce
225g (8oz) stir-fry vegetables, such as sliced courgettes, broccoli and green beans

 Swap

Instead of prawns, try chicken cut into strips; stir-fry for 5 minutes in step 1. Or, instead of raw prawns, use frozen cooked prawns.

STIR-FRIES

Nutritional Information (Per Serving)
170 calories, 7g fat (of which 1g saturates), 11g carbohydrate, 1.6g salt
Gluten free · Dairy free · Easy

Serves 2
Preparation time 4 minutes
Cooking time 5 minutes

135

Stir-fried Salmon and Broccoli

2 tsp sesame oil
1 red pepper, seeded and thinly sliced
½ red chilli, seeded and thinly sliced
   (see page 50)
1 garlic clove, peeled and crushed
125g (4oz) broccoli florets
2 spring onions, sliced
2 salmon fillets, about 125g (4oz)
   each, cut into strips
1 tsp Thai fish sauce
2 tsp soy sauce
wholewheat noodles to serve (see
   page 60)

1 Heat the oil in a wok or large frying pan. Add the red pepper, chilli, garlic, broccoli florets and spring onions and stir-fry over a high heat for 3–4 minutes.

2 Add the salmon fillets, Thai fish sauce and soy sauce, and cook for 2 minutes, stirring gently. Serve immediately with noodles.

 Moneysaver Tip
Instead of Thai fish sauce, season with a little salt.

Ready in under 30 minutes
Quick and easy
Healthy and sustaining
Brain food

STIR-FRIES

Serves 2
Preparation time 10 minutes
Cooking time 5–6 minutes

Nutritional Information (Per Serving)
90 calories, 4g fat (of which 1g saturates), 9g carbohydrate, 2.7g salt
Dairy free · Easy

Chicken Stir-fry with Noodles

1. Fill a large pan with water and bring to the boil. Meanwhile, heat the oil in a wok or frying pan, then add the garlic and stir-fry for 1–2 minutes. Add the chicken pieces and stir-fry for 5 minutes, then add the carrot strips and stir-fry for a further 5 minutes.

2. Put the noodles into the boiling water and cook according to the pack instructions.

3. Meanwhile, add the spring onions, mangetouts and sauce to the wok and stir-fry for 5 minutes.

4. Drain the cooked noodles well and add to the wok. Toss everything together and serve.

2 tbsp vegetable oil
2 garlic cloves, peeled and crushed
4 large skinless, boneless chicken thighs, each sliced into 10 pieces
3 medium carrots, peeled and cut into thin strips
250g pack thick egg noodles
1 bunch spring onions, sliced
200g (7oz) mangetouts, ends trimmed
155g jar sweet chilli and lemongrass sauce

**Healthy and sustaining
Comfort food**

STIR-FRIES

Nutritional Information (Per Serving)
355 calories, 10g fat (of which 2g saturates), 29g carbohydrate, 0.5g salt
Dairy free · Easy

Serves 4
Preparation time 20 minutes
Cooking time 20 minutes

137

Burgers, Sausages and Kebabs

Speedy Burgers

600g (1lb 5oz) minced beef
¼ onion, peeled and grated
1 tsp Worcestershire sauce
1–2 tsp vegetable oil
salt and ground black pepper

 1 Mix the mince with the onion and Worcestershire sauce and season well with salt and pepper. Shape into four rounds.

2 Heat the oil in a frying pan and cook the burgers, two at a time if necessary, for 5–6 minutes on each side.

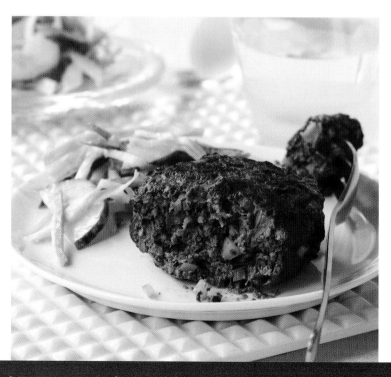

Ready in under 30 minutes
Quick and easy
Five ingredients or fewer
Comfort food

Makes 4
Preparation time 5 minutes
Cooking time 12–24 minutes

Nutritional Information (Per Serving)
353 calories, 26g fat (of which 11g saturates), 1g carbohydrate, 0.9g salt
Dairy free • Easy

Chicken Burgers

1 Put the chicken into a bowl with the shallots, tarragon, breadcrumbs and egg yolk. Mix well, then beat in about 75ml (3fl oz) cold water and season with salt and pepper.

2 Lightly oil a foil-lined baking sheet. Divide the chicken mixture into four portions and place on the foil. Using the back of a wet spoon, flatten each portion to a thickness of 2.5cm (1in). Cover and chill for 30 minutes.

3 Preheat the barbecue or grill. Cook the burgers for 5–6 minutes on each side or until cooked through, then serve in a toasted burger bun with a dollop of mayonnaise or Greek yogurt, a few salad leaves and tomato salad.

225g (8oz) minced chicken
2 shallots, peeled and finely chopped
1 tbsp freshly chopped tarragon
25g (1oz) fresh breadcrumbs
   (see step 1, page 131)
1 large egg yolk
oil to grease
salt and ground black pepper
burger buns, mayonnaise or Greek
   yogurt, salad leaves and tomato
   salad to serve

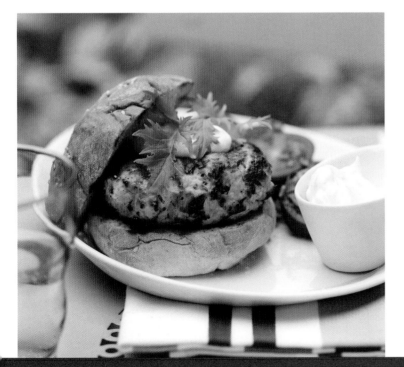

£ Moneysaver Tip
Instead of shallots use 1 onion.

Try Something Different
Pork and Apricot Burgers
Replace the chicken with minced pork, use chopped sage instead of tarragon and add 100g (3½oz) chopped ready-to-eat dried apricots to the mixture before shaping.

Healthy choice
Comfort food
Share with friends
Make in advance, cook later

BURGERS, SAUSAGES AND KEBABS

Nutritional Information (Per Serving)
205 calories, 4g fat (of which 1g saturates), 12g carbohydrate, 0.4g salt
Dairy free · Easy

Serves 2
Preparation time 30 minutes,
   plus 30 minutes chilling
Cooking time 12 minutes

Sausages: 3 Cooking Methods

Sausages come in loads of flavours and are easy to cook.

Fried sausages

Melt a little fat in a frying pan, add the sausages and fry for 15–20 minutes, keeping the heat low to prevent them burning and turning them once or twice to brown them evenly.

Grilled sausages

Heat the grill to hot, put the sausages on the grill rack in the grill pan and cook until one side is lightly browned, then turn them; continue cooking and turning them frequently for 15–20 minutes, until the sausages are well browned.

Baked sausages

Heat the oven to 200°C (180°C fan oven) mark 6. Put the sausages into a greased baking tin and cook in the centre of the oven for 30 minutes.

Quick Onion Gravy for Sausages

1 tbsp oil
1 red onion, peeled and finely sliced
1 tbsp plain flour
½ tsp tomato purée
1 beef stock cube
450ml (¾ pint) boiling water
2 bay leaves

 Heat the oil in a pan. Add the onion and fry for 10 minutes until soft. Stir in the flour and tomato purée and cook for 1 minute.

 Add the beef stock cube, water and bay leaves. Bring to the boil, then reduce the heat and simmer for 15 minutes. Season to taste with salt and pepper, remove the bay leaves and serve with sausages and mash.

BURGERS, SAUSAGES AND KEBABS

Serves 4, makes 450ml (¾ pint)
Preparation time 5 minutes
Cooking time 30 minutes

Nutritional Information (Per Serving)
64 calories, 3g fat (of which trace saturates), 9g carbohydrate, 0.6g salt
Dairy free · Easy

1 Cook the pasta in a pan of boiling water according to the pack instructions.

2 Put the sausages into a large non-stick pan with the onion and fry for 10 minutes until golden and cooked. Stir in the peperonata antipasto, basil and 1 tbsp lemon juice.

3 Drain the pasta, leaving about 2 tbsp cooking water, and put it back into the pan. Add the sausage sauce and the remaining lemon juice, then toss together and serve at once.

300g (11oz) dried pasta, such as
  fusilli
6 sausages, skinned and roughly
  chopped
1 large onion, peeled and finely
  chopped
290g jar peperonata antipasto
20g pack fresh basil, roughly chopped
1–2 tbsp lemon juice

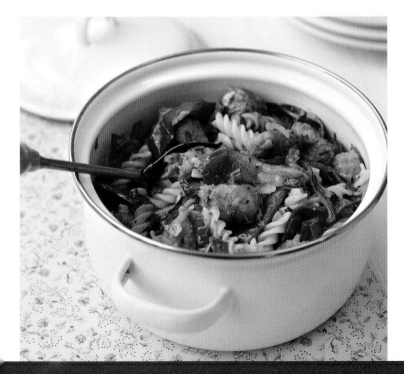

Ready in under **30 minutes**
Quick and easy
Comfort food
Share with friends

BURGERS, SAUSAGES AND KEBABS

Nutritional Information (Per Serving)
584 calories, 25g fat (of which 8g saturates), 75g carbohydrate, 3.1g salt
Dairy free • Easy

Serves 4
Preparation time 5 minutes
Cooking time about 10 minutes

Spicy Sausages

4 tbsp hot chilli sauce
4 tbsp clear honey
450g (1lb) coarse pork sausages
   (about 8)

1 Preheat the oven to 200°C (180°C fan oven) mark 6. Mix together the hot chilli sauce and honey.

2 Put the sausages into a small roasting tin and cook in the oven for about 10 minutes. Add the sauce and stir to coat the sausages on all sides. Cook for a further 20 minutes or until golden brown and cooked through. Serve with mashed potatoes (see page 56) or stir-fried vegetables (see page 67).

Five ingredients or fewer
Cheap eat
Comfort food
Share with friends

Serves 4
Preparation time 5 minutes
Cooking time 30 minutes

Nutritional Information (Per Serving)
414 calories, 26g fat (of which 10g saturates), 34g carbohydrate, 4.1g salt
Dairy free • Easy

Sausages and Fried Potatoes

1 Put the potatoes into a pan of lightly salted water, bring to the boil and par-boil for 10 minutes. Drain, then cut into 2.5cm (1in) cubes.

2 Heat the butter in a large frying pan. Add the onion and fry for 1 minute. Add the potatoes and fry over a medium heat for 25 minutes or until crisp and brown, turning frequently. Meanwhile, preheat the grill to medium-high.

3 Grill the sausages for about 20 minutes, turning from time to time, until browned and cooked through to the centre. Halfway through cooking, brush the onion rings with oil and add to the grill pan with the tomatoes. Grill until softened and lightly caramelised.

4 Serve the sausages on top of the potatoes, with the onion rings and tomatoes.

700g (1½lb) medium potatoes, unpeeled
50g (2oz) butter
1 small onion, peeled and chopped
450g (1lb) pork sausages
2 red onions, peeled and cut into rings
sunflower oil to brush
450g (1lb) small tomatoes
salt

Comfort food
Share with friends

Nutritional Information (Per Serving)
622 calories, 39g fat (of which 17g saturates), 51g carbohydrate, 3.3g salt
Easy

Serves 4
Preparation time 15 minutes
Cooking time 35 minutes

Sausages with Roasted
Potato and Onion Wedges

900g (2lb) large potatoes, peeled and cut into wedges
4 tbsp olive oil
3–4 fresh rosemary sprigs (if you like)
2 red onions, peeled and each cut into eight wedges
8 sausages
salt and ground black pepper

1 Preheat the oven to 220°C (200°C fan oven) mark 7. Put the potatoes into a roasting tin – they should sit in one layer. Drizzle the oil over them and season with salt and pepper. Toss well to coat the potatoes in oil, then put the rosemary on top, if you like, and roast in the oven for 20 minutes.

2 Remove the roasting tin from the oven (use oven gloves) and add the onion wedges. Toss again to coat the onions and potatoes. Put the sausages in between the potatoes and onions. Return the tin to the oven for 50 minutes–1 hour.

Timesaver Tip
Set the alarm on your mobile phone, or use a timer, and let the oven do the work while you get on with other things.

Swap
Instead of red onions, use white.

★ **Five ingredients or fewer**
Cheap eat
Comfort food
Share with friends

Serves 4
Preparation time 10 minutes
Cooking time 1 hour 20 minutes

Nutritional Information (Per Serving)
569 calories, 33g fat (of which 10g saturates), 53g carbohydrate, 2.8g salt
Dairy free • Easy

Potato and Sausage Skewers

1 Preheat the grill or barbecue. Soak twelve wooden skewers in water for 20 minutes. Boil the potatoes in lightly salted water for about 10 minutes or until almost tender. Drain well and toss with the oil, then season with salt and pepper.

2 Cut each sausage into three and thread on to the skewers alternately with the potatoes. Brush with oil and grill or barbecue for about 8 minutes, turning from time to time, until the sausages are cooked through and the potatoes begin to char.

3 Meanwhile, put the mint into a bowl, add the Parmesan and stir together until well mixed.

4 When the sausages are cooked, remove from the grill or barbecue and, while still hot, sprinkle with the mint and Parmesan mixture. Serve with rocket, if you like.

36 even-sized new potatoes, scrubbed
6 tbsp olive oil, plus extra to brush
12 thick sausages
2 tbsp freshly chopped mint
50g (2oz) freshly grated Parmesan
salt and ground black pepper
rocket to serve (if you like)

Cheap eat
Comfort food
Share with friends
Great for parties

Nutritional Information (Per Serving)
789 calories, 52g fat (of which 17g saturates), 58g carbohydrate, 4g salt
Easy

Serves 6
Preparation time 15 minutes
Cooking time 18 minutes

Mediterranean Kebabs

1 large courgette, trimmed and cut
    into chunks
1 red pepper, seeded and cut into
    chunks (see page 50)
12 cherry tomatoes
125g (4oz) halloumi cheese, cubed
100g (3½oz) natural yogurt
1 tsp ground cumin
2 tbsp olive oil
squeeze of lemon
1 lemon, cut into eight wedges
couscous tossed with freshly chopped
    flat-leafed parsley to serve (see Top
    Tip, page 257)

 Preheat the barbecue or grill. Soak eight wooden skewers in water for 20 minutes. Put the courgette into a large bowl with the red pepper, cherry tomatoes and halloumi cheese. Add the yogurt, cumin, olive oil and a squeeze of lemon and mix.

2 Push a lemon wedge on to each skewer, then divide the vegetables and cheese among the skewers. Grill the kebabs, turning regularly, for 8–10 minutes until the vegetables are tender and the halloumi is nicely charred. Serve with couscous.

★ **Ready in under 30 minutes**
Cheap eat
Share with friends
Great for parties

BURGERS, SAUSAGES AND KEBABS

Serves 4
Preparation time 15 minutes, plus
    soaking
Cooking time 8–10 minutes

Nutritional Information (Per Serving)
164 calories, 13g fat (of which 5g saturates), 7g carbohydrate, 1.1g salt
Vegetarian • Gluten free • Easy

Moroccan Spiced Chicken Kebabs

 1 Put the oil, parsley, garlic, paprika, cumin, lemon zest and juice into a bowl and use a stick blender to whiz to a paste.

2 Put the chicken into a shallow dish and add the spice paste, then rub in and leave to marinate for at least 20 minutes.

3 Preheat the barbecue or grill. Soak four wooden skewers in water for 20 minutes.

4 Thread the marinated chicken on to the skewers and grill for 10–12 minutes, turning every now and then, until cooked through. Serve with couscous salad and lime wedges.

2 tbsp olive oil
15g (½oz) flat-leafed parsley
1 garlic clove, peeled
½ tsp paprika
1 tsp ground cumin
grated zest and juice of 1 lemon
    (see Top Tip, page 93)
4 skinless chicken thighs, cut into
    bite-size chunks
couscous salad (see Top Tip, page
    257) and lime wedges to serve

Equipment Alert
You'll need a stick blender for this one.

Healthy choice
Cheap eat
Comfort food
Share with friends

BURGERS, SAUSAGES AND KEBABS

Nutritional Information (Per Serving)
189 calories, 5g fat (of which 1g saturates), 1g carbohydrate, 0.2g salt
Gluten free · Dairy free · Easy

Serves 4
Preparation time 10 minutes, plus
    minimum 20 minutes marinating
Cooking time 10–12 minutes

149

Spiced Tikka Kebabs

2 tbsp tikka paste
150g (5oz) natural yogurt
juice of ½ lime
4 spring onions, chopped
350g (12oz) boneless, skinless
    chicken thighs, cut into bite-size
    pieces
lime wedges to serve (if you like)

1 Preheat the grill. Put the tikka paste, yogurt, lime juice and chopped spring onions into a large bowl. Add the chicken and toss well. Thread the chicken on to skewers.

2 Grill for 8–10 minutes on each side or until cooked through, turning and basting with the paste. Serve with lime wedges to squeeze over the kebabs, if you like.

 Moneysaver Tips
- Instead of lime, use a lemon.
- Instead of boneless thighs, buy thighs on the bone and cut the meat off.

 Top Tip
Serve with **Rocket Salad**
Put 75g (3oz) rocket in a large bowl. Add ¼ chopped avocado, a handful of halved cherry tomatoes, ½ chopped cucumber and the juice of 1 lime or lemon. Season with salt and pepper and mix together.

Ready in under 30 minutes
Healthy choice
Comfort food
Share with friends

Serves 4
Preparation time 10 minutes
Cooking time 20 minutes

Nutritional Information (Per Serving)
150 calories, 5g fat (of which 1g saturates), 4g carbohydrate, 0.3g salt
Gluten free • Easy

Spiced Lamb in Pitta

1 Put the chopped pepper and onion into a bowl with the garlic, cumin and olive oil and use a stick blender to form a coarse paste. Add the chopped mint. Mix together the paste and the minced lamb, season with salt and pepper and shape into 16 patties. Chill for 30 minutes or overnight.

2 Put the tomatoes into a bowl, stir in the parsley and season with salt and pepper.

3 Preheat the barbecue, griddle or grill. Cook the lamb patties for 4–5 minutes on each side. Warm the pitta breads, wrap into a cone and secure with a cocktail stick. Fill each with four lamb patties and spoon on a drizzle of yogurt. Serve with the tomatoes and garnish with mint sprigs, if you like.

1 small green pepper, seeded and chopped (see page 50)
½ small onion, peeled and chopped
3 garlic cloves, peeled
2 tsp ground cumin
3 tbsp olive oil
1 tbsp freshly chopped mint
550g (1¼lb) lean minced lamb
450g (1lb) very ripe tomatoes, chopped
2 tbsp freshly chopped flat-leafed parsley
4 large pitta breads
salt and ground black pepper
Greek yogurt to serve
mint sprigs to garnish (if you like)

Equipment Alert
You'll need a stick blender for this one.

Freezing Tip
Complete the recipe to the end of step 1, place the patties on a tray to freeze, then wrap, label and freeze for up to one month.
To use Thaw at cool room temperature for four hours. Complete the recipe.

Comfort food
Share with friends
Great for parties
Make in advance, cook later

BURGERS, SAUSAGES AND KEBABS

Nutritional Information (Per Serving)
550 calories, 20g fat (of which 9g saturates), 60g carbohydrate, 1.3g salt
Easy

Serves 4
Preparation time 20 minutes, plus 30 minutes chilling
Cooking time 8–10 minutes

151

Pasta and Noodles

Quick Tomato Sauce

1 tbsp olive oil
1 small onion, peeled and finely
    chopped
1 garlic clove, peeled and chopped
400g can plum tomatoes
salt and ground black pepper

 Top Tip

Spaghetti with Tomato Sauce
While the sauce is simmering, cook
500g (1lb 2oz) spaghetti in a large
pan of boiling water (see Cooking
Pasta on page 59). Drain well,
reserving about a cup of the cooking
water. Return the pasta to the pan,
add the tomato sauce and mix well.
Add a splash or two of the cooking
water to loosen the pasta and sauce.
Grate some Cheddar cheese over
the pasta and season generously
with salt and black pepper.
Serves 4.

1 Heat the oil in a medium pan for 30 seconds, then add the onion and fry gently for 15 minutes, stirring regularly, until the onion is softened and translucent but not browned.

2 Add the garlic and continue to cook gently for 1 minute. Stir in the tomatoes. Fill the empty tomato can up to about half with cold water and give it a swirl to catch any tomato juice. Pour into the pan, then season with salt and pepper. Turn up the heat to medium and simmer the sauce for about 15 minutes or until it's thickened slightly.

Healthy choice
Five ingredients or fewer
Cheap eat
Comfort food

Serves 4
Preparation time 10 minutes
Cooking time 35 minutes

Nutritional Information (Per Serving) for Quick Tomato Sauce
46 calories, 3g fat (of which trace saturates), 4g carbohydrate, 0.7g salt
Vegetarian • Dairy free • Gluten free • Easy

Five Great Pasta Sauce Recipes
to make from the Quick Tomato Sauce

With tuna

Drain an 80g can of tuna in oil or brine (you can use some of the oil to cook the onion in step 1 of the sauce opposite). When the tomato sauce has thickened and finished simmering, stir in the drained tuna and cook for 2–3 minutes to warm through. Toss with pasta. Serves 4.

With bacon

Chop 2 rindless streaky bacon rashers and add to the pan with the onion at step 1 opposite. Cook for 10–15 minutes until the bacon is browned, then add the garlic and tomatoes and complete the recipe as above. Serves 4.

With red pepper and olives

Add 1 seeded and sliced red pepper (see page 50) to the pan when frying the onion at step 1 opposite, then complete the recipe as above. When the tomato sauce has finished simmering, add 6 pitted, chopped olives and cook for 1–2 minutes to heat through. Serves 4.

With chilli

Fry ½ finely chopped and seeded red chilli (see page 50) with the onion (or use ½ tsp dried chilli flakes), then complete the recipe as opposite. Serves 4.

With basil

After cooking the sauce, stir in a handful of freshly chopped basil. Serves 4.

Simple Meat Sauce

1. Heat the oil in a large pan, add the onion and fry over a medium heat for 15 minutes until softened and golden. Add the garlic and cook for 1 minute.

2. Add the mince and, as it browns, use a wooden spoon to break up the pieces. Stir the stock and tomato purée into the browned mince, cover the pan with a lid and bring to the boil. Add the tomatoes, Worcestershire sauce and mushrooms and season well with salt and pepper. Bring back to the boil, then reduce the heat and simmer, stirring occasionally, for 20 minutes.

Moneysaver Tip

Replace half the quantity of mince with 200g (7oz) red lentils and add them after browning the mince. There's no need to soak them, so just stir them in and complete the recipe.

Top Tips

You can use 1 beef stock cube dissolved in 300ml (½ pint) boiling water.

Spaghetti Bolognese

About 15 minutes before the sauce has finished cooking, cook 500g (1lb 2oz) spaghetti in a large pan of boiling water (see Cooking Pasta, page 59). Drain well, reserving about a cup of the cooking water. Return the pasta to the pan, add the meat sauce and mix well. Add a splash or two of the cooking water to loosen the pasta and sauce. Grate some Cheddar cheese over the pasta and serve.

Chilli Bolognese

To spice up the basic meat sauce, add ½ large red seeded chilli (see page 50) to the onion when frying in step 1.

1 tbsp olive oil
1 onion, peeled and finely chopped
2 garlic cloves, peeled and crushed
450g (1lb) minced beef
300ml (½ pint) beef stock (see Top Tips)
2 tbsp tomato purée
400g can chopped tomatoes
2 tbsp Worcestershire sauce
125g (4oz) button mushrooms, sliced
salt and ground black pepper

Cheap eat
Comfort food
Share with friends

Serves 4
Preparation time 15 minutes
Cooking time 40 minutes

Nutritional Information (Per Serving)
310 calories, 21g fat (of which 8g saturates), 6g carbohydrate, 2.5g salt
Dairy free · Easy

Six Quick Pasta Sauces

Lemon and Parmesan
Cook pasta shells in a large pan of lightly salted boiling water for the time stated on the pack. Add 125g (4oz) frozen peas to the pasta water for the last 5 minutes of the cooking time. Drain the pasta and peas, put back into the pan and add the grated zest and juice of ½ lemon and 75g (3oz) freshly grated Parmesan. Season with ground black pepper, toss and serve immediately.

Tomato, Prawn and Garlic
Put 350g (12oz) cooked peeled prawns into a bowl with 4 tbsp tomato purée and stir well. Heat 1 tbsp olive oil and 15g (½oz) butter in a frying pan and gently cook 3 peeled and sliced garlic cloves until golden. Add 4 large chopped tomatoes and 125ml (4fl oz) dry white wine. Leave the sauce to bubble for about 5 minutes, then stir in the prawns and some freshly chopped parsley.

Courgette and Anchovy
Heat the oil from a 50g can anchovies in a frying pan. Add 1 peeled and crushed garlic clove and a pinch of dried chilli and cook for 1 minute. Add 400ml (14fl oz) passata sauce (puréed and sieved tomatoes, available in jars), 2 diced courgettes and the anchovies. Bring to the boil, then reduce the heat and simmer for about 10 minutes, stirring well, until the anchovies have melted.

Broccoli and Thyme
Put 900g (2lb) trimmed broccoli into a pan with 150ml (¼ pint) hot vegetable stock. Bring to the boil, then cover and simmer for 3–4 minutes until tender – the stock should have evaporated. Add 2 peeled and crushed garlic cloves and 2 tbsp olive oil and cook for 1–2 minutes to soften the garlic. Add 250g carton mascarpone, 2 tbsp freshly chopped thyme and 100g (3½oz) freshly grated cheese and mix together. Season with salt and ground black pepper.

Quick and Easy Carbonara
Fry 150g (5oz) chopped smoked bacon rashers in 1 tbsp oil for 4–5 minutes. Add to drained, cooked pasta, such as tagliatelle, and keep hot. Put 2 large egg yolks into a bowl, add 150ml (¼ pint) double cream and whisk together. Add to the pasta with 50g (2oz) freshly grated Parmesan and 2 tbsp freshly chopped parsley.

Luxury Mushroom and Cream
Heat 1 tbsp olive oil in a large pan and fry 1 finely chopped onion for 7–10 minutes until soft. Add 300g (11oz) sliced mushrooms and cook for 3–4 minutes. Pour in 125ml (4fl oz) dry white wine and bubble for 1 minute, then stir in 500ml (18fl oz) low-fat crème fraîche. Heat until bubbling, then stir in 2 tbsp freshly chopped tarragon. Season with salt and ground black pepper.

Simple Chilli Pasta

350g (12oz) spaghetti
1 tbsp olive oil
2 garlic cloves, peeled and crushed
1 red chilli, seeded and chopped
(see page 50)
2 x 400g cans chopped tomatoes with
herbs
20g packet fresh basil
50g (2oz) pitted black olives

 1 Cook the spaghetti in a large pan of lightly salted boiling water according to the pack instructions. Drain and return to the pan.

 2 Meanwhile, heat the oil in another pan. Tip the garlic and chilli into the pan and fry for 2 minutes, stirring all the time. Add the tomatoes and cook for 5 minutes or until bubbling.

 3 Tear the basil leaves and add them to the tomatoes with the olives. Tip the mixture into the drained spaghetti, stir well and serve.

Ready in under **30 minutes**
Quick and easy
Healthy choice
Cheap eat

Serves 4
Preparation time 5 minutes
Cooking time about 10 minutes

Nutritional Information (Per Serving)
369 calories, 6g fat (of which 1g saturates), 71g carbohydrate, 0.9g salt
Vegetarian • Dairy free • Easy

Bacon, Chilli and Herb Pasta

 Cook the pasta in a large pan of lightly salted boiling water according to the pack instructions.

 Heat a large pan and fry the bacon for 3 minutes.

 Add the butter, sage and chilli, and cook for 30 seconds. Season with pepper.

4 Drain the pasta and tip into a bowl, then stir the sauce into the pasta and serve.

400g (14oz) dried fusilli pasta
150g (5oz) smoked streaky bacon, chopped
50g (2oz) butter
1 tbsp finely chopped fresh parsley or sage
½ red chilli, seeded and finely chopped (see page 50)
salt and ground black pepper

Ready in under 30 minutes
Five ingredients or fewer
Cheap eat
Comfort food

PASTA AND NOODLES

Nutritional Information (Per Serving)
545 calories, 21g fat (of which 10g saturates), 76g carbohydrate, 1.4g salt
Easy

Serves 4
Preparation time 5 minutes
Cooking time 10 minutes

Fusilli with Chilli
and Tomatoes

350g (12oz) fusilli or other short dried
    pasta
4 tbsp olive oil
1 large red chilli, seeded and finely
    chopped (see page 50)
1 garlic clove, peeled and crushed
500g (1lb 2oz) cherry tomatoes
2 tbsp freshly chopped basil
50g (2oz) Parmesan, shaved
    (see Top Tip)
salt and ground black pepper

 1 Cook the pasta in a large pan of lightly salted boiling water according to the pack instructions. Drain.

 2 Meanwhile, heat the oil in a large frying pan over a high heat. Add the chilli and garlic and cook for 30 seconds. Add the tomatoes, season with salt and pepper and cook over a high heat for 3 minutes or until the skins begin to split.

3 Add the basil and drained pasta and toss together. Transfer to a dish, sprinkle the Parmesan shavings over the top and serve immediately.

✅ Top Tip

Make Parmesan shavings with a vegetable peeler. Hold the piece of cheese in one hand and pare off wafer-thin strips of cheese using the peeler.

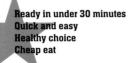
Ready in under **30 minutes**
Quick and easy
Healthy choice
Cheap eat

Serves 4
Preparation time 10 minutes
Cooking time 10–15 minutes

Nutritional Information (Per Serving)
479 calories, 17g fat (of which 4g saturates), 69g carbohydrate, 0.4g salt
Easy

Spicy Tomato Pasta

 1 Cook the pasta in a large pan of lightly salted boiling water according to the pack instructions.

 2 Drain the oil from the anchovies into a bowl and put 1 tbsp into a pan. Heat gently for 1 minute. Use the remaining oil for another recipe (see Top Tip).

3 Add the anchovies to the hot oil and cook for 1 minute. Add the tomatoes and simmer for 10 minutes. Stir in the olives and cook for 1–2 minutes more.

4 Drain the pasta, tip back into the pan and add the sauce. Toss together and serve with lemon wedges, if you like.

300g (11oz) chunky pasta shapes
50g jar anchovies in oil with garlic and herbs
6 tomatoes, chopped
75g (3oz) pitted black olives, chopped
1 lemon, cut into wedges (if you like)

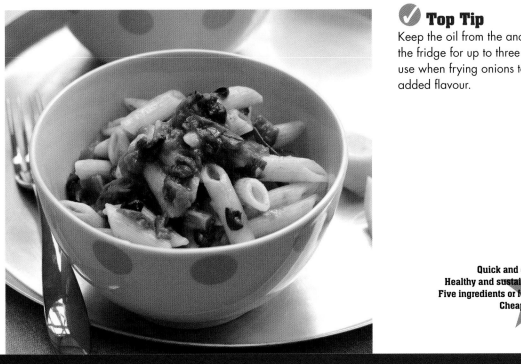

✔ Top Tip
Keep the oil from the anchovies in the fridge for up to three days and use when frying onions to give them added flavour.

Quick and easy
Healthy and sustaining
Five ingredients or fewer
Cheap eat

PASTA AND NOODLES

Nutritional Information (Per Serving)
343 calories, 7g fat (of which 1g saturates), 61g carbohydrate, 2g salt
Dairy free · Easy

Serves 4
Preparation time 5 minutes
Cooking time 15 minutes

Roast Tomato Pasta

400g (14oz) dried rigatoni pasta
700g (1½lb) cherry tomatoes
olive oil to drizzle
50g (2oz) pinenuts
a large handful of fresh basil leaves,
    torn
salt and ground black pepper
freshly grated Parmesan to serve

 Preheat the oven to 240°C (220°C fan oven) mark 9. Cook the pasta in a large pan of lightly salted boiling water according to the pack instructions.

 Meanwhile, cut half the tomatoes in two and arrange them in a large roasting tin, cut side up. Add the remaining whole tomatoes and drizzle all with oil. Season with salt and pepper. Put the pinenuts on to a separate roasting tray and roast both in the oven for 15 minutes until the tomatoes are softened and lightly caramelised. Watch carefully to make sure the pinenuts don't scorch and remove from the oven earlier if necessary.

3 Drain the pasta well and add to the roasting tin when the tomatoes are done. Scatter the basil and pinenuts over, then stir thoroughly to coat the pasta in the juices. Adjust the seasoning and stir in a little more oil, if you like. Sprinkle with Parmesan and serve.

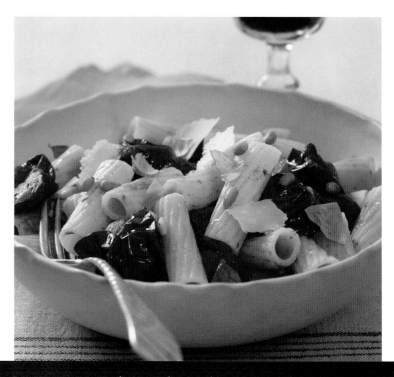

Ready in under 30 minutes
Quick and easy
Healthy choice

Serves 4
Preparation time 5 minutes
Cooking time 15 minutes

Nutritional Information (Per Serving)
507 calories, 16g fat (of which 2g saturates), 80g carbohydrate, 0g salt
Easy

Ham and Mushroom Pasta

 1 Cook the pasta in a large pan of lightly salted boiling water according to the pack instructions.

2 Meanwhile, heat the oil in a pan. Add the shallots and fry gently for 3 minutes until starting to soften. Add the mushrooms and fry for 5–6 minutes.

3 Drain the pasta, put back into the pan and add the shallots and mushrooms. Stir in the crème fraîche, ham and parsley. Toss everything together, season with salt and pepper and heat through to serve.

350g (12oz) penne pasta
1 tbsp olive oil
2 shallots, sliced
200g (7oz) small button mushrooms
3 tbsp crème fraîche
125g (4oz) smoked ham, roughly chopped
2 tbsp freshly chopped flat-leafed parsley
salt and ground black pepper

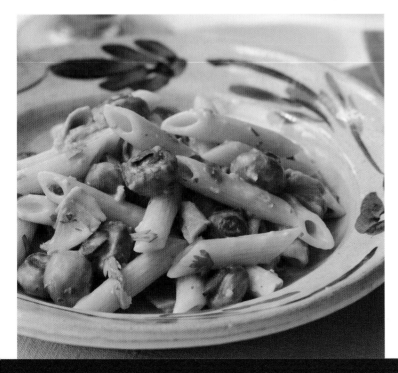

€ Moneysaver Tip

Instead of crème fraîche use cream or Greek yogurt.

Ready in under 30 minutes
Quick and easy
Cheap eat
Comfort food

PASTA AND NOODLES

Nutritional Information (Per Serving)
415 calories, 10g fat (of which 4g saturates), 67g carbohydrate, 1g salt
Easy

Serves 4
Preparation time 5 minutes
Cooking time 15 minutes

Pea, Mint and Ricotta Pasta

300g (11oz) farfalle pasta
200g (7oz) frozen peas
175g (6oz) ricotta cheese
3 tbsp freshly chopped mint
2 tbsp extra virgin olive oil
salt and ground black pepper

1 Cook the pasta in a large pan of lightly salted boiling water according to the pack instructions. Add the frozen peas for the last 4 minutes of cooking.

2 Drain the pasta and peas, reserving the water, then return to the pan. Stir in the ricotta and mint with a ladleful of pasta cooking water. Season well, drizzle with the oil and serve at once.

Ready in under 30 minutes
Quick and easy
Healthy choice
Five ingredients or fewer

Serves 4
Preparation time 5 minutes
Cooking time 10 minutes

Nutritional Information (Per Serving)
431 calories, 14g fat (of which 5g saturates), 63g carbohydrate, 0.2g salt
Vegetarian · Easy

Pasta with Pesto and Beans

 1 Bring a large pan of lightly salted water to the boil. Add the pasta, bring back to the boil and cook for 5 minutes.

2 Add the beans and potatoes to the pan and boil for a further 7–8 minutes until the potatoes are just tender.

3 Drain the pasta, beans and potatoes in a colander, then tip everything back into the pan and stir in the pesto. Serve scattered with Parmesan shavings.

350g (12oz) dried pasta shapes
175g (6oz) fine green beans, roughly chopped
175g (6oz) small salad potatoes, thickly sliced
250g (9oz) pesto (see Top Tip, page 98)
Parmesan shavings to serve (see Top Tip, page 160)

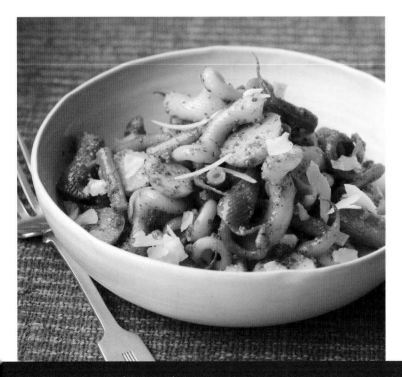

Moneysaver Tip

Use leftover cooked pasta, beans or potatoes: tip the pasta into a pan of boiling water and bring back to the boil for 30 seconds. Bring the beans or potatoes to room temperature, but there's no need to reboil them.

PASTA AND NOODLES

Nutritional Information (Per Serving)
738 calories, 38g fat (of which 10g saturates), 74g carbohydrate, 1g salt
Vegetarian · Easy

Serves 4
Preparation time 5 minutes
Cooking time 15 minutes

Fast Macaroni Cheese

300g (11oz) short-cut macaroni
drizzle of oil
1 quantity cheese sauce
  (see page 29)
freshly chopped flat-leafed parsley
  (if you like)
extra grated cheese to sprinkle
salt and ground black pepper

1 Preheat the grill to high. Cook the macaroni in a large pan of lightly salted boiling water according to the pack instructions. Drain well, then put into a 1.1 litre (2 pint) ovenproof dish. Add a drizzle of oil, season well and stir to mix. Stir in the cheese sauce, and the parsley, if you like.

2 Sprinkle the grated cheese over the macaroni. Put under the grill for 5 minutes or until golden brown on top and bubbling. Serve immediately.

Serves 4
Preparation time 5 minutes
Cooking time 15 minutes

Nutritional Information (Per Serving)
215 calories, 11g fat (of which 6g saturates), 21g carbohydrate, 1.1g salt
Vegetarian • Easy

Chicken, Bacon and Leek
Pasta Bake

1 Heat the oil in a large frying pan. Add the bacon and chicken and cook for 7–8 minutes. Add the leeks and continue cooking for 4–5 minutes.

2 Meanwhile, cook the pasta in a large pan of lightly salted boiling water according to the pack instructions. Drain well.

3 Preheat the grill. Add the cheese sauce to the pasta with the mustard, chicken mixture and parsley. Mix well, then tip into a 2.1 litre (3¾ pint) ovenproof dish and sprinkle with Parmesan. Grill for 4–5 minutes until golden.

1 tbsp olive oil
100g (3½oz) chopped streaky bacon rashers
450g (1lb) boneless, skinless chicken thighs, chopped
3 medium leeks, trimmed and chopped
300g (11oz) macaroni or other pasta shapes
350g carton ready-made cheese sauce
2 tsp Dijon mustard
2 tbsp freshly chopped flat-leafed parsley
25g (1oz) freshly grated Parmesan

£ Moneysaver Tips

- Instead of boneless chicken thighs, buy thighs on the bone and cut the meat off.
- Make home-made cheese sauce (see page 29).

Nutritional Information (Per Serving)
650 calories, 24g fat (of which 6g saturates), 68g carbohydrate, 2.2g salt
Easy

Serves 4
Preparation time 10 minutes
Cooking time about 20 minutes

Hot Noodle Salad

250g pack medium egg noodles
2 tsp groundnut oil
2 × 300g packs stir-fry vegetables
  (see Moneysaver Tip)
1 tsp crushed chilli flakes
4 eggs, beaten
roughly chopped peanuts, freshly
  chopped coriander and lime
  wedges to serve (if you like)

 1 Put the egg noodles into a bowl of boiling water and leave to soak for 5 minutes. Drain well.

 2 Meanwhile, heat the oil in a large wok over a high heat. Add the vegetables and chilli flakes and stir-fry for 3–4 minutes. Season the eggs with salt and pepper and pour over the vegetables. Cook for 1–2 minutes to let the egg set on the bottom, then stir in the noodles.

 3 Serve with roughly chopped peanuts, freshly chopped coriander and lime wedges to squeeze over the top, if you like.

£ Moneysaver Tip

When you're on a budget,
ready-prepared vegetables
can be expensive. Chop up
your own veg and save money.

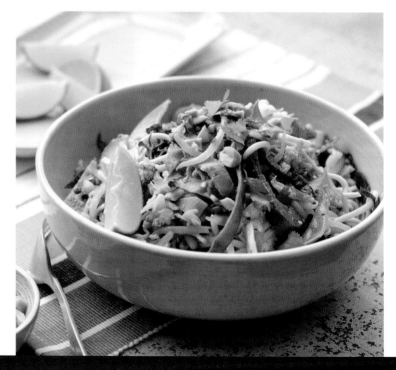

Serves 4
Preparation time 10 minutes
Cooking time 5–7 minutes

Nutritional Information (Per Serving)
396 calories, 14g fat (of which 4g saturates), 52g carbohydrate, 0.5g salt
Vegetarian • Dairy free • Easy

Thai Noodles with Tofu

1. Preheat the oven to 200°C (180°C fan oven) mark 6. Put the tofu and shallots into a small roasting pan. Put the garlic, ginger, soy sauce, vinegar and 2 tbsp water into a bowl and stir well. Pour the mixture over the tofu and shallots and toss well to coat. Roast near the top of the oven for 30 minutes until the tofu and shallots are golden.

2. Meanwhile, soak the noodles according to the pack instructions. Drain, refresh under cold running water and set aside. Toast and chop the peanuts.

3. To make the sauce, put all the ingredients into a small pan and stir over a gentle heat until the sugar dissolves. Keep the sauce warm.

4. Heat the oil in a wok or large frying pan and stir-fry the dried shrimp, if using, for 1 minute. Add the drained noodles and beaten egg to the pan and stir over a medium heat for 3 minutes. Add the tofu and shallots, together with any pan juices. Stir well, then remove from the heat.

5. Stir in the bean sprouts and the sauce, then divide among four warmed serving plates. Sprinkle with the toasted peanuts and serve immediately, garnished with basil leaves.

125g (4oz) firm tofu, drained and cut
 into 2.5cm (1in) cubes
8 shallots, peeled and halved
1 garlic clove, peeled and crushed
2.5cm (1in) piece fresh root ginger,
 peeled and grated
2 tbsp soy sauce
1 tsp white wine vinegar or
 rice vinegar
225g (8oz) rice noodles
25g (1oz) unsalted peanuts
2 tbsp sunflower oil
15g (½oz) dried shrimp (if you like)
1 medium egg, beaten
25g (1oz) bean sprouts
fresh basil leaves to garnish (if you like)

FOR THE SAUCE
1 dried red chilli, seeded and finely
 chopped
2 tbsp lemon juice
1 tbsp Thai fish sauce
1 tbsp caster sugar
2 tbsp smooth peanut butter

PASTA AND NOODLES

Nutritional Information (Per Serving)
431 calories, 15g fat (of which 3g saturates), 61g carbohydrate, 2.1g salt
Dairy free · Easy

Serves 4
Preparation time 25 minutes
Cooking time 35 minutes

169

Chicken Chow Mein

250g (9oz) medium egg noodles
1 tbsp toasted sesame oil
2 boneless, skinless chicken breasts or
large thighs, cut into thin strips
1 bunch of spring onions, thinly sliced
diagonally
150g (5oz) mangetouts, thickly sliced
diagonally
125g (4oz) bean sprouts
100g (3½oz) cooked ham, shredded
120g sachet chow mein sauce
salt and ground black pepper
light soy sauce to serve

1 Cook the noodles in boiling water for 4 minutes or according to the pack instructions. Drain, rinse thoroughly in cold water, drain again and set aside.

2 Meanwhile, heat a wok or large frying pan until hot, then add the oil. Add the chicken and stir-fry over a high heat for 3–4 minutes until browned all over. Add the spring onions and mangetouts, stir-fry for 2 minutes, then stir in the bean sprouts and ham and cook for a further 2 minutes.

3 Add the drained noodles, then pour in the chow mein sauce and toss together to coat evenly. Stir-fry for 2 minutes or until piping hot. Season with salt and pepper and serve immediately with light soy sauce to drizzle over.

 Moneysaver Tips
- Instead of boneless chicken, use chicken pieces and cut the meat off.
- Instead of mangetouts use frozen peas.

Ready in under 30 minutes
Healthy and sustaining
Five ingredients or fewer
Share with friends

Serves 4
Preparation time 10 minutes
Cooking time 10 minutes

Nutritional Information (Per Serving)
451 calories, 11g fat (of which 2g saturates), 59g carbohydrate, 1.3g salt
Dairy free • Easy

Quick Pad Thai

1 Put the noodles into a heatproof bowl, cover with boiling water and soak for 4 minutes until softened. Drain, rinse under cold water and set aside.

2 Heat a wok or large frying pan until hot, add the chilli pesto and stir-fry for 1 minute. Add the mangetouts and sugarsnap peas and cook for a further 2 minutes. Tip into a bowl. Put the pan back on the heat, add the eggs and cook, stirring, for 1 minute.

3 Add the soy sauce, prawns and noodles to the pan. Toss well and cook for 3 minutes until piping hot. Return the vegetables to the pan, cook for a further 1 minute until heated through, then sprinkle with the peanuts. Serve with extra soy sauce and lime wedges to squeeze over, if you like.

250g (9oz) wide ribbon rice noodles
3 tbsp satay and sweet chilli pesto
125g (4oz) mangetouts, thinly sliced
125g (4oz) sugarsnap peas, thinly sliced
3 medium eggs, beaten
3 tbsp chilli soy sauce, plus extra to serve
250g (9oz) cooked peeled tiger prawns
25g (1oz) dry-roasted peanuts, roughly crushed
lime wedges to serve (if you like)

£ Moneysaver Tips

- Instead of satay and sweet chilli pesto, substitute 2 tbsp peanut butter and 1 tbsp sweet chilli sauce.
- Chilli soy sauce can be replaced with 2 tbsp light soy sauce and ½ red chilli, finely chopped (see page 50).
- Instead of tiger prawns use small frozen cooked prawns.
- Instead of mangetouts and sugar snap peas, use frozen peas.

Ready in under 30 minutes
Healthy and sustaining
Comfort food
Share with friends

PASTA AND NOODLES

Nutritional Information (Per Serving)
451 calories, 13g fat (of which 3g saturates), 56g carbohydrate, 2.6g salt
Dairy free · Easy

Serves 4
Preparation time 12 minutes, plus 4 minutes soaking
Cooking time 8 minutes

Pork and Noodle Stir-fry

1 tbsp sesame oil
5cm (2in) piece fresh root ginger,
    peeled and grated
2 tbsp soy sauce
1 tbsp fish sauce
½ red chilli, finely chopped
    (see page 50)
450g (1lb) stir-fry pork strips
2 red peppers, seeded and roughly
    chopped (see page 50)
250g (9oz) baby sweetcorn, halved
    lengthways
200g (7oz) sugarsnap peas, halved
300g (11oz) bean sprouts
250g (9oz) rice noodles

1 Put the sesame oil into a large bowl. Add the ginger, soy sauce, fish sauce, chilli and pork strips. Mix well and leave to marinate for 10 minutes.

2 Heat a wok or large frying pan until hot. Lift the pork out of the marinade with a slotted spoon and add it to the pan. Stir-fry over a high heat for 5 minutes. Add the peppers, sweetcorn, sugarsnap peas, bean sprouts and remaining marinade and stir-fry for a further 2–3 minutes until the pork is cooked.

3 Meanwhile, soak the noodles for 4 minutes or according to the pack instructions.

4 Drain the noodles, add them to the pan and toss well. Serve immediately.

£ Moneysaver Tips
- Instead of fish sauce, season with a little salt to taste.
- Instead of sugarsnap peas, use frozen peas.

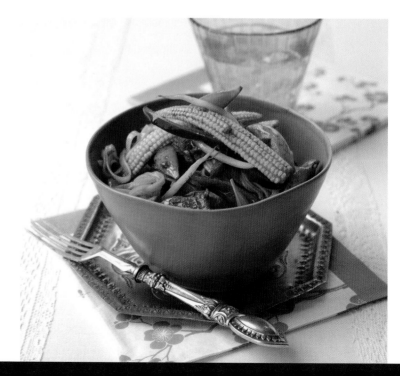

PASTA AND NOODLES

Serves 4
Preparation time 15 minutes, plus
    marinating
Cooking time 7–8 minutes

Nutritional Information (Per Serving)
476 calories, 8g fat (of which 2g saturates), 64g carbohydrate, 3.4g salt
Dairy free · Easy

Sesame Beef

1 Put the soy sauce and Worcestershire sauce, tomato purée, lemon juice, sesame seeds and garlic into a bowl. Add the steak and toss to coat.

2 Heat the oil in a large wok or non-stick frying pan until hot. Add the steak and sear well. Remove from the wok and set aside.

3 Add any sauce from the bowl to the wok and heat for 1 minute. Add the pak choi, spring onions and steak and stir-fry for 5 minutes. Add freshly cooked and drained noodles, toss and serve immediately.

2 tbsp soy sauce
2 tbsp Worcestershire sauce
2 tsp tomato purée
juice of ½ lemon
1 tbsp sesame seeds
1 garlic clove, crushed
400g (14oz) rump steak, sliced
1 tbsp vegetable oil
3 small pak choi, chopped
1 bunch of spring onions, sliced
freshly cooked egg noodles or
    tagliatelle to serve

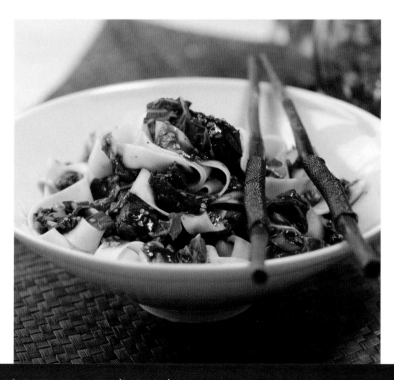

£ Moneysaver Tips

- Instead of rump steak, use frying steak.
- Instead of pak choi, use Chinese leaves or shredded spring greens or cabbage.

⟳ Swap

Use 400g (14oz) pork escalope cut into strips instead of beef. Cook for 5 minutes before removing from the pan at step 2.

Ready in under 30 minutes
Healthy and sustaining
Comfort food
Share with friends

PASTA AND NOODLES

Nutritional Information (Per Serving)
207 calories, 10g fat (of which 3g saturates), 4g carbohydrate, 2g salt
Dairy free · Easy

Serves 4
Preparation time 10 minutes
Cooking time 10 minutes

Rice and Grains

Simple Fried Rice

Curried Vegetable Rice

Tomato Risotto

Spiced Chicken Pilau

Spiced Egg Pilau

Quinoa with Mint Dressing

Stuffed Tomatoes

Griddled Polenta with Cheese Salad

Very Easy Four Cheese Gnocchi

Pesto Gnocchi

Simple Fried Rice

150g (5oz) long-grain white rice
2 tbsp sesame oil
3 medium eggs, lightly beaten
250g (9oz) frozen peas
250g (9oz) cooked peeled prawns
salt

1 Cook the rice in boiling water for about 10 minutes or according to the pack instructions. Drain well.

2 Heat 1 tsp sesame oil in a large non-stick frying pan. Pour in half the beaten eggs and tilt the pan around over the heat for about 1 minute until the egg is set. Tip the omelette on to a warm plate. Repeat with another 1 tsp sesame oil and the remaining beaten egg to make another omelette. Tip on to another warm plate.

3 Add the remaining oil to the pan and stir in the rice and peas. Stir-fry for 2–3 minutes until the peas are cooked. Stir in the prawns.

4 Roll up the omelettes, roughly chop one-third of one, then slice the remainder into strips. Add the chopped omelette to the rice, peas and prawns and cook for 1–2 minutes until heated through. Divide the fried rice among four bowls, top with the sliced omelette and serve immediately.

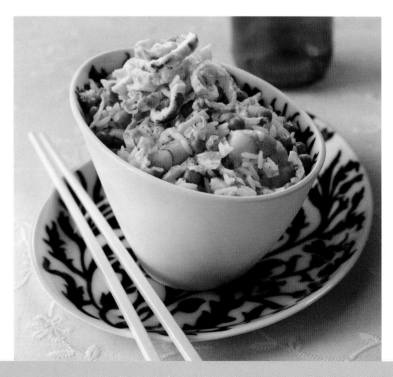

Ready in under 30 minutes
Quick and easy
Five ingredients or fewer
Cheap eat

Serves 4
Preparation time 5 minutes
Cooking time 15–20 minutes

Nutritional Information (Per Serving)
339 calories, 11g fat (of which 2g saturates), 37g carbohydrate, 0.4g salt
Gluten free · Dairy free · Easy

Curried Vegetable Rice

1 Heat the oil in a large pan and fry the onion for 15 minutes until tender.

2 Add the curry paste and cook for 2–3 minutes.

3 Add the carrot and rice to the onion and curry paste, then immediately add the stock and plenty of seasoning. Cover the pan and bring to the boil, then reduce the heat and simmer for 10 minutes.

4 Add the broccoli or cauliflower florets and cook for 5 minutes, then serve.

1 tbsp vegetable oil
1 small onion, peeled and chopped
½ tsp Balti curry paste
1 large carrot, peeled and grated
150g (5oz) long-grain rice
300ml (½ pint) chicken or vegetable stock (see Top Tip)
handful of broccoli or cauliflower florets (see page 52)
salt and ground black pepper

 Top Tip
You can use 1 vegetable or chicken stock cube dissolved in 300ml (½ pint) boiling water.

Cheap eat
Comfort food
Share with friends

RICE AND GRIANS

Nutritional Information (Per Serving)
384 calories, 8g fat (of which 1g saturates), 74g carbohydrate, 2.2g salt
Gluten free · Dairy free · Easy

Serves 2
Preparation time 5 minutes
Cooking time 35 minutes

177

Tomato Risotto

1 large fresh rosemary sprig
2 tbsp olive oil
1 small onion, peeled and finely
    chopped
350g (12oz) risotto (arborio) rice
4 tbsp dry white wine (if you have it)
750ml (1¼ pints) hot vegetable stock
    (see Top Tip)
300g (11oz) cherry tomatoes, halved
salt and ground black pepper
shavings of Parmesan (see Top Tip
    page 160), green salad and extra
    virgin olive oil to serve

1 Pull the leaves from the rosemary and chop roughly. Set aside.

2 Heat the oil in a flameproof casserole, add the onion and cook for 8–10 minutes until beginning to soften. Add the rice and stir to coat in the oil and onion. Pour in the wine, if you have it, then the hot stock, stirring well to mix.

3 Bring to the boil, stirring, then cover and simmer for 5 minutes. Stir in the tomatoes and chopped rosemary. Simmer, covered, for a further 10–15 minutes until the rice is tender and most of the liquid has been absorbed. Season to taste.

4 Serve immediately with shavings of Parmesan, a large green salad and extra virgin olive oil to drizzle over.

✔ Top Tip
You can use 1½ vegetable stock cubes dissolved in 750ml (1¼ pints) boiling water.

Healthy and sustaining
Five ingredients or fewer
Cheap eat
Comfort food

Serves 6
Preparation time 10 minutes
Cooking time 25–30 minutes

Nutritional Information (Per Serving)
264 calories, 4g fat (of which 1g saturates), 49g carbohydrate, 0.5g salt
Gluten free • Easy

Spiced Chicken Pilau

1. Spread the pinenuts over a baking sheet and toast under a hot grill until golden brown, turning them frequently. Put to one side.

2. Heat the oil in a large heavy-based pan over a medium heat. Add the onions and garlic and cook for 5 minutes until soft. Remove half the onion mixture and put to one side.

3. Add the curry powder and cook for 1 minute, then add the chicken and stir. Cook for 10 minutes if the meat is raw, or for 4 minutes if you're using cooked chicken, stirring from time to time until browned.

4. Add the rice, stir to coat in the oil, then add 900ml (1½ pints) boiling water, the salt and saffron. Cover and bring to the boil. Reduce the heat to low and cook for 20 minutes or until the rice is tender and most of the liquid has been absorbed. Stir in the reserved onion mixture, the sultanas, tomatoes and pinenuts. Cook for 5 minutes to warm through, then serve.

50g (2oz) pinenuts
2 tbsp olive oil
2 onions, peeled and sliced
2 garlic cloves, peeled and crushed
2 tbsp medium curry powder
6 boneless, skinless chicken thighs or 450g (1lb) skinless cooked chicken, cut into strips
350g (12oz) American easy-cook rice
2 tsp salt
pinch of saffron threads
50g (2oz) sultanas
225g (8oz) ripe tomatoes, roughly chopped

£ Moneysaver Tips

- Instead of pinenuts, use unsalted cashew nuts or cashew pieces.
- You can omit the saffron.

Healthy and sustaining
Five ingredients or fewer
Comfort food
Share with friends

Nutritional Information (Per Serving)
649 calories, 18g fat (of which 2g saturates), 87g carbohydrate, 2.8g salt
Gluten free · Dairy free · Easy

Serves 4
Preparation time 15 minutes
Cooking time 35–40 minutes

Spiced Egg Pilau

200g (7oz) basmati rice, soaked and
 rinsed
150g (5oz) frozen peas
4 medium eggs
200ml (7fl oz) coconut cream
1 tsp mild curry paste
1 tbsp sweet chilli sauce
1 tbsp smooth peanut butter
1 large bunch fresh coriander, roughly
 chopped
mini poppadums and mango chutney
 to serve (if you like)

1 Put the rice into a pan with 450ml (¾ pint) boiling water and cook according to the pack instructions until just tender. Add the frozen peas for the last 5 minutes of cooking time.

2 Meanwhile, put the eggs into a large pan of boiling water and simmer for 6 minutes, then drain, run under cold water and shell when cool enough to handle.

3 Put the coconut cream, curry paste, chilli sauce and peanut butter into a small pan and whisk together. Heat the sauce gently, stirring, without allowing it to boil.

4 Drain the rice and stir in the chopped coriander and 2 tbsp of the sauce.

5 Divide the rice among four bowls. Cut the eggs into halves and serve on the rice, spooning the remaining coconut sauce over the top. Serve with poppadums and chutney, if you like.

Quick and easy
Healthy and sustaining
Five ingredients or fewer
Cheap eat

Serves 4
Preparation time 5 minutes
Cooking time 15 minutes

Nutritional Information (Per Serving)
331 calories, 9g fat (of which 12g saturates), 50g carbohydrate, 0.6g salt
Vegetarian · Gluten free · Dairy free · Easy

Quinoa with Mint Dressing

1　Cook the quinoa in a pan with the stock for 15 minutes or until tender (or according to the pack instructions). Drain thoroughly and put into a bowl.

2　Add the spring onions and mint to the bowl with the toasted pinenuts, lemon juice and olive oil. Stir until well mixed and season lightly. Serve with kebabs, grilled poultry, fish or shellfish.

250g (9oz) quinoa, rinsed (see page 64)
400ml (14fl oz) hot vegetable or chicken stock (see Top Tip)
4 spring onions, finely chopped
20g (¾oz) mint, finely chopped
25g (1oz) pinenuts, toasted
2 tbsp lemon juice
3 tbsp olive oil
salt and ground black pepper

✔ Top Tip
You can use 1 vegetable or chicken stock cube dissolved in 400ml (14fl oz) boiling water.

Quick and easy
Healthy and sustaining
Cheap eat
Comfort food

RICE AND GRIANS

Nutritional Information (Per Serving)
264 calories, 13g fat (of which 2g saturates), 33g carbohydrate, 0g salt
Vegetarian · Gluten free · Dairy free · Easy

Serves 4
Preparation time 10 minutes
Cooking time 15 minutes

181

Stuffed Tomatoes

125g (4oz) bulgur wheat (see page 64)
20g (¾oz) flat-leafed parsley, finely chopped
75g (3oz) feta cheese, chopped
1 courgette, trimmed and chopped
50g (2oz) flaked almonds, toasted (see Top Tip)
4 large beef tomatoes
1 tbsp olive oil

 Preheat the oven to 180°C (160°C fan oven) mark 4. Cook the bulgur according to the pack instructions. Chop the parsley, feta and courgette and stir into the bulgur with the almonds.

Chop the top off each tomato and scoop out the seeds. Put the tomatoes on a baking sheet and spoon in the bulgur mixture. Drizzle with the oil and cook in the oven for 15–20 minutes until the cheese is starting to soften.

 Top Tip

To toast almonds, put them into a dry frying pan and heat gently for a few minutes, stirring occasionally, until they start to brown. Don't leave them – they burn quickly. Take them off the heat – they will continue to brown as they cool.

 Swap

Try quinoa (see page 64) instead of the bulgur wheat.

Healthy choice

Serves 4
Preparation time 10 minutes
Cooking time 30–35 minutes

Nutritional Information (Per Serving)
245 calories, 14g fat (of which 4g saturates), 21g carbohydrate, 0.7g salt
Vegetarian · Easy

Griddled Polenta
with Cheese Salad

1 Lightly oil a baking tray. Pour the milk into a pan, then add the sage, 1 scant tsp salt and 300ml (½ pint) water and bring to the boil. Add the polenta to the pan in a thin, steady stream, stirring, to make a smooth paste.

2 Reduce the heat, add the garlic and cook for about 8 minutes, stirring occasionally. Add the oil, then season with pepper and stir well. Pour into the prepared tray, smooth the top and leave to cool for 45 minutes.

3 Once the polenta is cool, turn out on to a board and cut into eight pieces. You can make this in advance.

4 Melt the butter in a griddle pan and fry the polenta slices on each side until golden.

5 Divide among four plates. Add the salad, cheese, sunblush tomatoes and peppers and serve.

2 tbsp olive oil, plus extra to grease
300ml (½ pint) semi-skimmed milk
10 fresh sage leaves, roughly chopped
125g (4oz) quick-cook polenta
2 garlic cloves, peeled and crushed
25g (1oz) butter
100g (3½oz) salad leaves
125g (4oz) cheese, cut into cubes (Gorgonzola is good)
125g (4oz) each sunblush tomatoes and roasted red peppers
salt and ground black pepper

£ **Moneysaver Tip**
Instead of fresh sage, use 1 tsp dried.

Healthy and sustaining
Comfort food
Share with friends
Make in advance, cook later

RICE AND GRAINS

Nutritional Information (Per Serving)
362 calories, 22g fat (of which 11g saturates), 28g carbohydrate, 1.1g salt
Vegetarian • Gluten free • Easy

Serves 4
Preparation time 20 minutes, plus 45 minutes cooling
Cooking time 15 minutes

183

Very Easy Four Cheese
Gnocchi

2 tsp salt
2 x 350g packs fresh gnocchi
500g tub fresh four-cheese sauce
2 x 240g packs sunblush tomatoes
4 tbsp torn basil leaves
2 tbsp freshly grated Parmesan cheese
25g (1oz) butter, chopped
salt and ground black pepper

1 Bring two large pans of water to the boil, add 1 tsp salt and 1 pack gnocchi to each and cook for the time stated on the pack or until all the pieces have floated to the surface. Drain well and put back into one pan.

2 Preheat the grill. Pour the cheese sauce and tomatoes over the gnocchi and heat gently, stirring, for 2 minutes. Season, then add the basil and stir again. Put into individual heatproof bowls, sprinkle the Parmesan over and dot with the butter. Grill for 3–5 minutes or until golden and bubbling, then serve.

Ready in under 30 minutes
Quick and easy
Comfort food
Share with friends

Serves 4
Preparation time 2 minutes
Cooking time 20 minutes

Nutritional Information (Per Serving)
580 calories, 24g fat (of which 12g saturates), 75g carbohydrate, 0.5g salt
Vegetarian · Easy

Pesto Gnocchi

1 Cook the gnocchi in a large pan of lightly salted boiling water according to the pack instructions. Add the beans to the water for the last 3 minutes of cooking time.

2 Drain the gnocchi and beans and put back into the pan. Add the pesto and tomatoes and toss well. Serve immediately.

2 x 350g packs fresh gnocchi
200g (7oz) green beans, trimmed and chopped
125g (4oz) pesto (see Top Tip, page 98)
10 sunblush tomatoes, roughly chopped

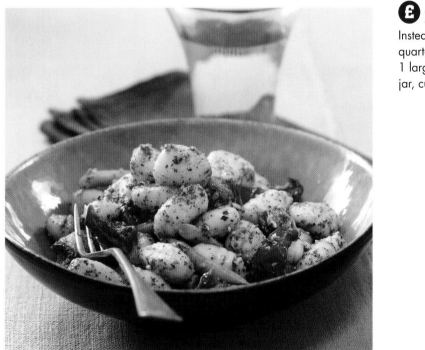

£ Moneysaver Tip

Instead of sunblush tomatoes, use quartered cherry tomatoes, or 1 large roasted red pepper from a jar, cut into pieces.

Ready in under 30 minutes
Five ingredients or fewer
Cheap eat
Comfort food

RICE AND GRIANS

Nutritional Information (Per Serving)
481 calories, 24g fat (of which 6g saturates), 56g carbohydrate, 0.4g salt
Vegetarian • Easy

Serves 4
Preparation time 10 minutes
Cooking time 10 minutes

185

Beans and Lentils

Mushroom and Bean Hotpot

3 tbsp olive oil
700g (1½ lb) chestnut mushrooms,
   roughly chopped
1 large onion, peeled and finely
   chopped
2 tbsp plain flour
2 tbsp mild curry paste
150ml (¼ pint) hot vegetable stock
   (see Top Tip)
400g can chopped tomatoes
2 tbsp sun-dried tomato paste
2 x 400g cans mixed beans, drained
   and rinsed
3 tbsp mango chutney
3 tbsp roughly chopped fresh
   coriander and mint

1. Heat the oil in a large pan over a low heat and fry the mushrooms and onion until the onion is soft and dark golden. Stir in the flour and curry paste and cook for 1–2 minutes, then add the hot stock, tomatoes, sun-dried tomato paste and beans.

2. Bring to the boil, then simmer gently for 30 minutes or until most of the liquid has reduced. Stir in the chutney and herbs before serving.

£ Moneysaver Tips

- Instead of chestnut mushrooms, use white mushrooms.
- Use fresh parsley instead of corander and mint.

✔ Top Tip

You can use ½ vegetable stock cube dissolved in 150ml (¼ pint) boiling water.

**Healthy and sustaining
Cheap eat
Comfort food
Share with friends**

BEANS AND LENTILS

Serves 6
Preparation time 15 minutes
Cooking time 30 minutes

Nutritional Information (Per Serving)
244 calories, 8g fat (of which 1g saturates), 35g carbohydrates, 2g salt
Vegetarian · Dairy free · Easy

Black-eyed Bean Chilli

1. Heat the oil in a frying pan. Add the onion and celery and cook for 10 minutes until softened.

2. Add the beans, tomatoes and Tabasco sauce to the pan. Bring to the boil, then reduce the heat and simmer for 10 minutes.

3. Just before serving, stir in the coriander. Spoon the chilli on to the warm tortillas, roll up and serve with soured cream.

1 tbsp olive oil
1 onion, peeled and chopped
3 celery sticks, finely chopped
2 x 400g cans black-eyed beans, drained and rinsed
2 x 400g cans chopped tomatoes
2 or 3 splashes of Tabasco sauce
3 tbsp freshly chopped coriander
4 warmed tortillas and soured cream to serve

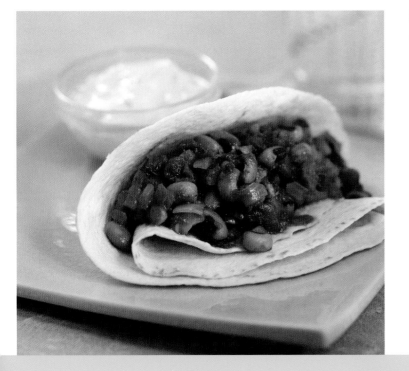

£ Moneysaver Tips

- Instead of soured cream, use yogurt.
- Use parsley instead of coriander.

Quick and easy
Healthy and sustaining
Cheap eat
Comfort food

BEANS AND LENTILS

Nutritional Information (Per Serving)
245 calories, 5g fat (of which 1g saturates), 39g carbohydrate, 1.8g salt
Vegetarian · Easy

Serves 4
Preparation time 10 minutes
Cooking time 20 minutes

189

Chickpea Patties

2 x 400g cans chickpeas, drained
  and rinsed
4 garlic cloves, peeled and crushed
1 tsp ground cumin
1 small red onion, peeled and finely
  chopped
20g pack fresh coriander, chopped
2 tbsp plain flour, plus extra to dust
olive oil for frying
mixed salad and lemon wedges
  to serve

1 Pat the chickpeas dry with kitchen paper then mash them with the garlic, cumin, onion and coriander. Stir in the flour.

2 With floured hands, shape the chickpea mixture into 12 small, round patties and chill in the fridge for 20 minutes.

3 Heat a little oil in a non-stick frying pan over a medium heat and fry the patties in batches for about 2 minutes on each side or until heated through and golden. Serve warm with mixed salad and lemon wedges.

Healthy choice
Cheap eat
Comfort food
Share with friends

Serves 4
Preparation time 20 minutes, plus chilling
Cooking time about 15 minutes

Nutritional Information (Per Serving)
344 calories, 17g fat (of which 2g saturates), 37g carbohydrate, 1g salt
Dairy free · Easy

Chickpea and Chilli Stir-fry

1   Heat the oil in a wok. Add the ground cumin and fry for
    1–2 minutes. Add the onion and stir-fry for 5–7 minutes.

2   Add the garlic and chilli and stir-fry for 2 minutes.

3   Add the chickpeas to the wok with the tomatoes. Reduce the heat
    and simmer until the chickpeas are hot. Add the spinach and stir
    to wilt. Serve with brown rice or pasta.

2 tbsp olive oil
1 tsp ground cumin
1 red onion, peeled and sliced
2 garlic cloves, peeled and finely
    chopped
1 red chilli, seeded and finely
    chopped (see page 50)
2 x 400g cans chickpeas, drained
    and rinsed
400g (14oz) cherry tomatoes
125g (4oz) baby spinach leaves
brown rice or pasta to serve (see
    pages 61 and 59)

£ Moneysaver Tips

- Instead of red onion, use white.
- Use shredded spinach instead of baby spinach.

Ready in under 30 minutes
Quick and easy
Healthy and sustaining
Cheap eat

BEANS AND LENTILS

Nutritional Information (Per Serving)
258 calories, 11g fat (of which 1g saturates), 30g carbohydrate, 1g salt
Vegetarian · Dairy free · Gluten free

Serves 4
Preparation time 10 minutes
Cooking time 15–20 minutes

Hot Spiced Chickpeas

1 tbsp oil
1 onion, peeled and chopped
2 tsp ground turmeric
1 tbsp cumin seeds
450g (1lb) tomatoes, roughly chopped
2 x 400g cans chickpeas, drained
    and rinsed
1 tbsp lemon juice
4 tbsp freshly chopped coriander
fresh coriander leaves to garnish
    (if you like)
salt and ground black pepper

1 Heat the oil in a pan. Add the onion and cook for 5–10 minutes until golden brown, stirring constantly.

2 Add the turmeric and cumin seeds and cook, stirring, for 1–2 minutes. Add the tomatoes and chickpeas to the pan together with the lemon juice, coriander and seasoning. Cook for 1–2 minutes, stirring frequently.

3 Garnish with coriander leaves, if you like, and serve with baked potatoes, rice or wholemeal bread.

£ Moneysaver Tip
Instead of coriander, use parsley.

Ready in under 30 minutes
Quick and easy
Healthy and sustaining
Cheap eat

BEANS AND LENTILS

Serves 4
Preparation time 5 minutes
Cooking time 10–15 minutes

Nutritional Information (Per Serving)
201 calories, 7g fat (of which 1g saturates), 27g carbohydrate, 0.7g salt
Vegetarian • Gluten free • Dairy free • Easy

Warm Tofu, Fennel
and Bean Salad

1 Heat 1 tbsp oil in a large frying pan. Add the onion and fennel, and cook over a medium heat for 5–10 minutes until soft.

2 Add the vinegar and heat through for 2 minutes. Stir in the butter beans and parsley, season with salt and pepper, then tip into a bowl.

3 Slice the smoked tofu into four, then into eight triangles. Add to the pan with the remaining oil. Cook for 2 minutes on each side or until golden.

4 Divide the bean mixture among four plates and add two slices of tofu to each plate

1 tbsp olive oil, plus 1 tsp
1 red onion, peeled and finely sliced
1 fennel bulb, finely sliced
1 tbsp cider or white wine vinegar
400g can butter beans, drained
    and rinsed
2 tbsp freshly chopped flat-leafed
    parsley
200g (7oz) smoked tofu
salt and ground black pepper

£ Moneysaver Tips
- Instead of red onion, use white.
- Instead of fennel, use white cabbage.

Ready in under 30 minutes
Quick and easy
Healthy choice
Cheap eat

BEANS AND LENTILS

Nutritional Information (Per Serving)
150 calories, 6g fat (of which 1g saturates), 15g carbohydrate, 0.8g salt
Vegetarian · Gluten free · Dairy free · Easy

Serves 4
Preparation time 10 minutes
Cooking time 15 minutes

Warm Lentil Salad

2 medium eggs
2 tsp olive oil
2 small leeks, chopped
4 spring onions, chopped
1 red pepper, seeded and chopped
   (see page 50)
400g can lentils, drained and rinsed
150ml (¼ pint) vegetable stock
   (see Top Tip)
a handful of rocket or lettuce leaves
salt and ground black pepper

1 Gently lower the eggs into a pan of boiling water and simmer for 7 minutes.

2 Meanwhile, heat the olive oil in a separate pan and fry the leeks, spring onions and red pepper for 6–8 minutes until softened.

3 Stir in the lentils and stock and bring to the boil, then reduce the heat and simmer for 1–2 minutes. Peel the eggs, then cut in half. Season the lentil mixture with salt and pepper, then divide between two bowls and top each with an egg and a few rocket leaves.

✔ Top Tip

You can use ½ vegetable stock cube dissolved in 150ml (¼ pint) boiling water.

Ready in under 30 minutes
Healthy choice
Cheap eat
Brain food

Serves 2
Preparation time 15 minutes
Cooking time 10 minutes

Nutritional Information (Per Serving)
300 calories, 10g fat (of which 2g saturates), 33g carbohydrate, trace salt
Vegetarian • Gluten free • Dairy free • Easy

Warm Lentil and Egg Salad

1. Heat the oil in a large pan. Add the onion, carrot and celery and cook for 5 minutes. Add the peppers and mushrooms. Cover and cook for a further 5 minutes. Stir in the lentils and stock. Bring to the boil and simmer, covered, for 25–30 minutes.

2. Meanwhile, bring a large pan of water to the boil. Break the eggs into the water and cook for 3–4 minutes. Lift them out with a slotted spoon, drain on kitchen paper and keep warm.

3. A couple of minutes before the end of the lentil cooking time, add the spinach and cook until wilted. Stir in the vinegar. Spoon on to four plates or bowls and top each with a poached egg. Season with pepper and serve.

1 tbsp olive oil
1 onion, 1 carrot and 1 celery stick, finely chopped
2 red peppers, seeded and roughly chopped (see page 50)
200g (7oz) flat mushrooms, sliced
200g (7oz) brown lentils, rinsed and drained
600ml (1 pint) hot vegetable stock (see Top Tip)
4 medium eggs
100g (3½ oz) baby spinach leaves
2 tbsp balsamic vinegar
ground black pepper

£ Moneysaver Tip
Instead of baby spinach leaves, use shredded spinach.

✓ Top Tip
You can use 1 vegetable stock cube dissolved in 600ml (1 pint) boiling water.

Healthy and sustaining
Cheap eat
Brain food
Comfort food

BEANS AND LENTILS

Nutritional Information (Per Serving)
317 calories, 10g fat (of which 2g saturates), 37g carbohydrate, 0.7g salt
Vegetarian • Gluten free • Dairy free • Easy

Serves 4
Preparation time 15 minutes
Cooking time 35–40 minutes

195

Chicken and Fish Suppers

One-pot Chicken Thighs
Easy Chicken and Vegetable Hotpot
Chicken and Leek Pie
Spicy Chicken Wings
Sticky Chicken Thighs
Fried Chicken
One-pan Chicken with Tomatoes
Chicken, Bean and Spinach Curry
Garlic and Thyme Chicken
Lemon Chicken
Sticky Chicken Wings
Bacon and Tuna Hash
Grilled Sardines with Harissa
Sardines with Med Veg
Peppered Mackerel
Smoked Mackerel with Potato and Horseradish Salad

One-pot Chicken Thighs

8 chicken thighs, skin removed
2 tbsp chicken seasoning
1 onion, peeled and chopped
1 garlic clove, peeled and crushed
2 tbsp vegetable oil
2 tbsp light muscovado sugar
900g (2lb) potatoes, peeled and
   cut into small chunks
450g (1lb) carrots, peeled and
   cut into small chunks
600ml (1 pint) chicken stock
   (see Top Tip)
400g can chopped tomatoes
400g can chickpeas, drained
   and rinsed
salt and ground black pepper

1 Put the chicken into a large dish and season generously. Sprinkle the chicken seasoning over the chicken, turning the chicken to coat evenly, then stir in the onion and garlic. You can cook the chicken straight away or cover and chill it for several hours until needed. This will improve the flavour.

2 Take a large heavy-based pan and add the oil and sugar. Cook on a medium heat for 3 minutes until it turns a rich golden caramel colour, making sure it doesn't burn.

3 Without wasting a second, add the seasoned chicken – stand back, as the fat may splatter. Cook, without stirring, for 5 minutes, then turn the chicken over and cook for a further 5 minutes until it is evenly browned.

4 Add the potatoes and carrots to the pan, stir together well and cook for 5 minutes. Pour 600ml (1 pint) boiling water into a measuring jug and crumble in the stock cube. Stir to mix, then add to the chicken with the tomatoes. Cover and simmer gently for 20 minutes, then add the chickpeas and cook for 5 minutes.

✓ Top Tip
You can use 1 chicken stock cube dissolved in 600ml (1 pint) boiling water.

Comfort food
Share with friends
Great for parties

Serves 4
Preparation time 20 minutes
Cooking time 45 minutes

Nutritional Information (Per Serving)
600 calories, 23g fat (of which 5g saturates), 71g carbohydrate, 3.3g salt
Dairy free · Easy

Easy Chicken and Vegetable Hotpot

1 Heat a non-stick frying pan or flameproof casserole until hot. Add the chicken breasts, skin side down, and cook for 5–6 minutes. Turn them over and add the parsnips and carrots. Cook for a further 7–8 minutes.

2 Pour the gravy over the chicken and vegetables, then cover and cook gently for 10 minutes.

3 Season with pepper and stir in the cabbage, then cover and continue to cook for 4–5 minutes until the chicken is cooked through, the cabbage has wilted and the vegetables are tender. Serve hot.

4 chicken breasts, with skin, about 125g (4oz) each
2 large parsnips, chopped
2 large carrots, chopped
300ml (½ pint) ready-made gravy
125g (4oz) cabbage, shredded
ground black pepper

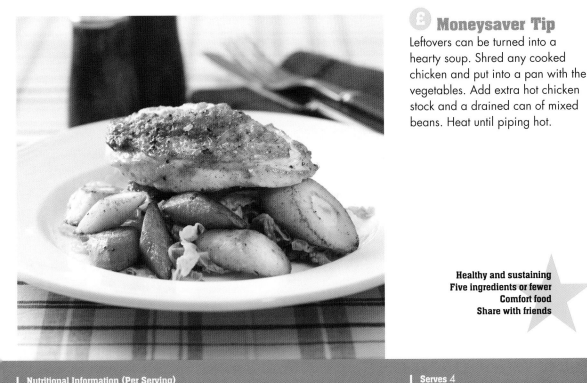

Moneysaver Tip
Leftovers can be turned into a hearty soup. Shred any cooked chicken and put into a pan with the vegetables. Add extra hot chicken stock and a drained can of mixed beans. Heat until piping hot.

Healthy and sustaining
Five ingredients or fewer
Comfort food
Share with friends

CHICKEN AND FISH SUPPERS

Nutritional Information (Per Serving)
338 calories, 14g fat (of which 3g saturates), 14g carbohydrate, 1.2g salt
Dairy free • Easy

Serves 4
Preparation time 5 minutes
Cooking time 30 minutes

Chicken and Leek Pie

5 large potatoes, peeled and chopped
    into chunks
200g (7oz) crème fraîche
3 large chicken thighs, with skin,
    about 125g (4oz) each
3 large leeks, trimmed and chopped
    into chunks
about 10 fresh tarragon leaves, finely
    chopped
salt and ground black pepper

1 Preheat the oven to 200°C (180°C fan oven) mark 6. Put the potatoes into a pan of lightly salted cold water. Cover, bring to the boil and simmer for 10–12 minutes until soft. Drain and put back into the pan. Add 1 tbsp crème fraîche, season with salt and pepper and mash well.

2 Meanwhile, heat a frying pan, add the chicken, skin side down, and fry gently for 5 minutes or until the skin is golden. Turn the chicken over and fry for 6–8 minutes. Remove the chicken from the pan and put on to a board. Tip the leeks into the pan and cook in the juices over a low heat for 5 minutes to soften.

3 Discard the chicken skin and cut the flesh into bite-size pieces (don't worry if it is not quite cooked through). Put the chicken back into the pan, stir in the remaining crème fraîche and heat for 2–3 minutes until bubbling. Stir in the tarragon, season with salt and pepper, then spoon into a 1.7 litre (3 pint) ovenproof dish. Spread the mash on top and cook in the oven for 20–25 minutes until golden and heated through. Serve hot.

Moneysaver Tip
Instead of fresh tarragon, use ½ tsp dried.

Five ingredients or fewer
Comfort food
Share with friends

Serves 4
Preparation time 15 minutes
Cooking time 40–45 minutes

Nutritional Information (Per Serving)
591 calories, 23g fat (of which 15g saturates), 54g carbohydrate, 0.3g salt
Gluten free · Easy

Spicy Chicken Wings

1 Preheat the oven to 200°C (180°C fan oven) mark 6. Put the harissa, cumin and oil into a bowl and mix well.

2 Add the chicken wings and brush with the mixture. Put into a roasting tin and roast in the oven for 30–35 minutes until golden and tender.

3 Serve with lemon wedges, if you like, to squeeze over, and a salad.

1 tbsp harissa paste (see Top Tip)
2 tsp ground cumin
1 tbsp olive oil
8 chicken wings
lemon wedges for squeezing
   (if you like)
salad to serve

Top Tip

Harrissa is a a spicy paste flavoured with chillies, coriander and caraway. You can use it with poultry, meat and fish, either when grilled, baked or in stews, so if you like spicy food, you will probably find plenty of uses for this North African spice blend. It's quite cheap to buy from supermarkets.

Healthy choice
Five ingredients or fewer
Share with friends
Great for parties

Nutritional Information (Per Serving)
758 calories, 50g fat (of which 14g saturates), 0g carbohydrate, 0.6g salt
Gluten free · Dairy free · Easy

Serves 4
Preparation time 5 minutes
Cooking time 30–35 minutes

Sticky Chicken Thighs

1 garlic clove, peeled and crushed
1 tbsp clear honey
1 tbsp Thai sweet chilli sauce
4 chicken thighs
green salad to serve

 Preheat the oven to 200°C (180°C fan oven) mark 6. Put the garlic into a bowl with the honey and chilli sauce and mix together. Add the chicken thighs and toss to coat.

2 Put into a roasting tin and roast for 15–20 minutes until the chicken is golden and cooked through. Serve with a crisp green salad.

Try Something Different
Try this with sausages instead of the chicken.

Italian Marinade
Mix 1 peeled and crushed garlic clove with 4 tbsp olive oil, the juice of 1 lemon and 1 tsp dried oregano. If you like, leave to marinate for 1–2 hours before cooking.

Oriental Marinade
Mix together 2 tbsp soy sauce, 1 tsp demerara sugar, 2 tbsp apple juice, 1 tsp finely chopped fresh root ginger and 1 peeled and crushed garlic clove.

Honey and Mustard
Mix together 2 tbsp grain mustard, 3 tbsp clear honey and the grated zest and juice of 1 lemon (see Top Tip, page 93).

Ready in under 30 minutes
Five ingredients or fewer
Cheap eat
Comfort food

Serves 4
Preparation time 5 minutes
Cooking time 20 minutes

Nutritional Information (Per Serving)
218 calories, 12g fat (of which 3g saturates), 5g carbohydrate, 0.4g salt
Gluten free • Dairy free • Easy

Fried Chicken

1 Wipe the chicken joints and pat dry with kitchen paper. Season with salt and pepper.

2 Toss the chicken in the flour until completely coated.

3 Heat the butter or oil in a large frying pan over a high heat. Add the chicken and cook until golden brown on both sides. Reduce the heat and cook for 30–40 minutes until tender. Drain on kitchen paper. Serve with a green salad, if you like.

4 chicken joints or pieces
3 tbsp plain flour
50g (2oz) butter or 3 tbsp
   vegetable oil
salt and ground black pepper
green salad to serve (if you like)

 Top Tip

To make sure that the chicken stays moist, the surface should be browned at a high temperature to seal in all the juices and give a good colour; the heat should then be reduced for the remaining cooking time.

Five ingredients or fewer
Comfort food
Share with friends

CHICKEN AND FISH SUPPERS

Nutritional Information (Per Serving)
565 calories, 42g fat (of which 10g saturates), 9g carbohydrate, 0.5g salt
Easy

Serves 4
Preparation time 5 minutes
Cooking time 35–45 minutes

One-pan Chicken
with Tomatoes

4 chicken thighs
1 red onion, peeled and sliced
400g can chopped tomatoes with
    herbs
400g can mixed beans, drained
    and rinsed
2 tsp balsamic vinegar
freshly chopped flat-leafed parsley
    to garnish (if you like)

1 Heat a non-stick pan and fry the chicken thighs, skin side down, until golden. Turn over and fry for 5 minutes.

2 Add the onion and fry for 5 minutes. Add the tomatoes, mixed beans and vinegar, cover and simmer for 10–12 minutes until piping hot. Garnish with chopped parsley, if you like, and serve immediately.

 Swap

Use flageolet, cannellini or haricot beans, or other canned beans, instead of mixed beans.

 Top Tip

If you don't have a non-stick pan, fry the chicken in 2 tbsp vegetable oil.

Quick and easy
Five ingredients or fewer
Cheap eat
Comfort food

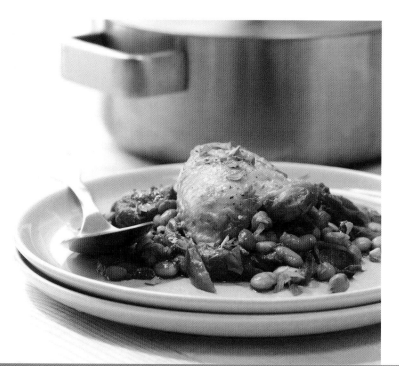

Serves 4
Preparation time 5 minutes
Cooking time 20–25 minutes

Nutritional Information (Per Serving)
238 calories, 4g fat (of which 1g saturates), 20g carbohydrate, 1g salt
Gluten free · Dairy free · Easy

Chicken, Bean and Spinach Curry

1 Heat the oil in a large pan over a medium heat and fry the chicken strips with the garlic until golden. Add the curry sauce, beans and apricots, then cover and simmer gently for 15 minutes or until the chicken is tender.

2 Over a low heat, stir in the yogurt, keeping the curry hot without boiling it, then stir in the spinach until it just begins to wilt. Add a spoonful of yogurt and serve with naan bread.

1 tbsp sunflower oil
350g (12oz) boneless, skinless chicken thighs, cut into strips
1 garlic clove, peeled and crushed
300–350g tub or jar curry sauce
400g can aduki beans, drained and rinsed
175g (6oz) ready-to-eat dried apricots
150g (5oz) natural yogurt, plus extra to serve
125g (4oz) baby spinach leaves
naan bread to serve

Moneysaver Tips
- Instead of baby spinach leaves, use shredded spinach.
- You could even make a very cheap vegetarian version using just the canned aduki beans. Use 2 cans to serve 4.

Healthy and sustaining
Comfort food
Share with friends
Great for parties

Nutritional Information (Per Serving)
358 calories, 11g fat (of which 2g saturates), 38g carbohydrate, 2.9g salt
Gluten free · Easy

Serves 4
Preparation time 10 minutes
Cooking time about 20 minutes

Garlic and Thyme Chicken

2 garlic cloves, peeled and crushed
2 tbsp freshly chopped thyme leaves
2 tbsp olive oil
4 chicken thighs
salt and ground black pepper

1 Preheat the barbecue or grill. Mix together the garlic, thyme and olive oil in a large bowl. Season with salt and pepper.

2 Using a sharp knife, make two or three slits in each chicken thigh. Put the chicken into the bowl and toss to coat thoroughly in the flavoured oil. Grill for 5–7 minutes on each side until golden and cooked through.

Moneysaver Tip
Use chicken thighs on the bone with skin. They're cheaper than the skinless version and the skin will keep the chicken succulent, which is especially useful if you're cooking them on the barbecue.

Quick and easy
Healthy choice
Five ingredients or fewer
Cheap eat

Serves 4
Preparation time 10 minutes
Cooking time 10–15 minutes

Nutritional Information (Per Serving)
135 calories, 6g fat (of which 1g saturates), trace carbohydrate, 0.2g salt
Gluten free · Dairy free · Easy

Lemon Chicken

1. Put the chicken into a large bowl and season with salt. Add the lemon juice and oil and stir to mix.

2. Preheat the grill to medium. Spread the chicken out on a large baking sheet and sprinkle with 2–3 tbsp demerara sugar. Grill for 3–4 minutes until caramelised, then turn the chicken over, sprinkle with the remaining sugar and grill until the chicken is golden and cooked through.

3. Divide the chicken among four plates and serve with a green salad and lemon wedges.

4 small boneless, skinless chicken breasts or large thighs, about 125g (4oz) each
juice of 2 lemons
2 tbsp olive oil
4–6 tbsp demerara sugar
salt
green salad and lemon wedges to serve

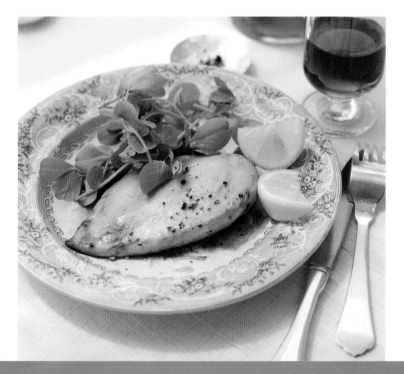

Quick and easy
Healthy choice
Five ingredients or fewer
Comfort food

Nutritional Information (Per Serving)
231 calories, 7g fat (of which 1g saturates), 13g carbohydrate, 0.2g salt
Gluten free · Dairy free · Easy

Serves 4
Preparation time 2 minutes
Cooking time 6–8 minutes

Sticky Chicken Wings

4 tbsp clear honey
4 tbsp wholegrain mustard
12 large chicken wings
salt and ground black pepper
grilled corn on the cob and green
   salad to serve (if you like)

1 Put the honey and mustard into a large glass dish and mix together. Add the chicken wings and toss to coat. Season well with salt and pepper. Cook immediately or, if you've time, cover, chill and leave to marinate for about 2 hours.

2 Preheat the barbecue or preheat a grill. Lift the wings from the marinade and cook for 8–10 minutes on each side until cooked through. Or you can roast them in a preheated oven 200°C (180°C fan oven) mark 6 for 40–45 minutes. Serve hot, with grilled corn and a green salad, if you like.

Try Something Different

Hoisin, Sesame and Orange Marinade
Mix together 6 tbsp hoisin sauce, 1 tbsp sesame seeds and the juice of ½ orange. Add the chicken wings and toss to coat.

Middle Eastern Marinade
Mix together 3 tbsp harissa paste (see Top Tip, page 201), 1 tbsp tomato purée and 3 tbsp olive oil. Stir in a small handful each of freshly chopped mint and parsley, add the chicken wings and toss to coat.

Healthy and sustaining
Five ingredients or fewer
Cheap eat
Comfort food

Serves 4
Preparation time 10 minutes, plus 2 hours marinating (optional)
Cooking time 20–45 minutes

Nutritional Information (Per Serving)
257 calories, 14g fat (of which 4g saturates), 13g carbohydrate, 0.5g salt
Gluten free · Dairy free · Easy

Bacon and Tuna Hash

1 Put the potatoes into a pan of lightly salted water, bring to the boil, then reduce the heat and simmer, partially covered, for 5–10 minutes or until beginning to soften. Drain and set aside.

2 Melt the butter in a non-stick frying pan, add the bacon and cook on a medium heat until beginning to brown, then add the onion. Cook for 5 minutes or until soft. Add the potatoes, and olives if you like, reduce the heat and cook for 10 minutes.

3 Using a spatula, turn the hash over and continue to cook for a further 10 minutes, turning every now and again. Add the tuna and cook for a further 4–5 minutes or until the potatoes are done to the centre and the tuna is hot. Season to taste and serve.

450g (1lb) new potatoes, cut into small chunks
25g (1oz) butter
125g (4oz) streaky bacon rashers, cut into 2.5cm (1in) strips
1 large onion, peeled and roughly chopped
125g (4oz) pitted green or black olives (if you like)
200g can tuna in oil, drained and flaked
salt and ground black pepper

Healthy choice
Cheap eat
Brain food
Comfort food

CHICKEN AND FISH SUPPERS

Nutritional Information (Per Serving)
359 calories, 21g fat (of which 7g saturates), 23g carbohydrate, 3.8g salt
Gluten free · Easy

Serves 4
Preparation time 10 minutes
Cooking time 35 minutes

Grilled Sardines with Harissa

1 garlic clove, peeled and crushed
2 tbsp olive oil
1–2 tsp harissa paste (see Top Tip, page 201)
4 whole sardines
salt and ground black pepper
tomato salad, watercress and lime wedges to serve (if you like)

 Preheat the grill to high. Put the garlic into a bowl. Add the oil and harissa paste, season to taste with salt and pepper and mix together.

 Slash the sardines a couple of times on each side, then brush the harissa and oil mixture all over. Grill for 5–10 minutes on each side until cooked through.

3 Serve with tomato salad, watercress and lime wedges to squeeze over the sardines, if you like.

✅ Top Tip

Oily fish such as sardines are one of the best sources of essential heart-protecting omega-3 oils. Eat them at least once a week.

Ready in under 30 minutes
Healthy choice
Five ingredients or fewer
Brain food

Serves 2
Preparation time 10 minutes
Cooking time 10–20 minutes

Nutritional Information (Per Serving)
292 calories, 21g fat (of which 4g saturates), 2g carbohydrate, 0.3g salt
Gluten free • Dairy free • Easy

Sardines with Med Veg

1 Heat the oil in a large frying pan or preheat the grill. Add the onions and fry for 2–3 minutes until almost soft. Add the garlic and peppers and stir-fry for 5 minutes, then add the courgettes and stir-fry for 4–5 minutes until almost soft. Remove from the pan and keep warm.

2 Season the sardines and cook in the pan or under a hot grill for 3–4 minutes on each side until cooked in the centre.

3 Drizzle the sardines with a little olive oil and lemon juice. Garnish with basil, if you like, and serve with the vegetables.

3 tbsp olive oil
2 red onions, peeled, halved and cut into petals
2 garlic cloves, peeled and crushed
2 red peppers, seeded and cut into chunks (see page 50)
225g (8oz) courgettes, trimmed and cut into small chunks
900g (2lb) sardines (about 16), cleaned
olive oil and lemon juice to drizzle
salt and ground black pepper
small fresh basil sprigs to garnish (if you like)

Healthy choice
Cheap eat
Brain food
Comfort food

Nutritional Information (Per Serving)
409 calories, 23g fat (of which 5g saturates), 13g carbohydrate, 0.5g salt
Gluten free • Dairy free • Easy

Serves 4
Preparation time 15 minutes
Cooking time 20 minutes

Peppered Mackerel

4 tsp whole mixed peppercorns
4 fresh mackerel, gutted, about
    250g (9oz) each (see Top Tips)
1 tbsp sunflower oil
200ml (7fl oz) crème fraîche
lemon wedges to garnish and green
    vegetables to serve (if you like)

1 Lightly crush 2 tsp of the peppercorns. Sprinkle one side of each mackerel with half the crushed peppercorns.

2 Heat the oil in a frying pan over a medium-high heat. Add the fish, peppered side down, and cook for 5–7 minutes. Sprinkle the mackerel with the remaining crushed peppercorns, turn the fish over and continue to fry for 5–7 minutes until cooked (see Top Tips). Remove and keep warm.

3 Wipe out the pan, add the crème fraîche and bring to the boil. Stir in the remaining whole peppercorns. (If the sauce becomes too thick, add some boiling water.)

4 To serve, spoon the sauce over the mackerel, garnish with lemon wedges and serve with green vegetables.

 Top Tips

- If the mackerel are large, make three shallow slashes on either side of the fish.
- To test whether the fish is cooked, prise the flesh from the backbone with a knife; it should be opaque and come away easily.

Ready in under 30 minutes
Healthy choice
Five ingredients or fewer
Brain food

Serves 4
Preparation time 10 minutes
Cooking time 15 minutes

Nutritional Information (Per Serving)
764 calories, 63g fat (of which 22g saturates), 1g carbohydrate, 0.4g salt
Gluten free • Easy

Smoked Mackerel
with Potato and Horseradish Salad

1 Cook the potatoes in a pan of lightly salted boiling water for 15–20 minutes until tender. Drain and set aside.

2 In a bowl, mix together the horseradish sauce, crème fraîche, lemon juice and oil, then season with pepper.

3 Roughly chop the apples and the warm potatoes, put into a large bowl and toss in the dressing. Skin and flake the mackerel and add to the bowl with the watercress. Toss together and serve.

350g (12oz) new potatoes, scrubbed
2 tbsp horseradish sauce
2 tbsp crème fraîche
1 tbsp lemon juice
4 tbsp olive oil
2 crisp apples, cored
2 smoked mackerel fillets
100g (3½oz) watercress
ground black pepper

 Swap

- Use wholegrain Dijon mustard instead of horseradish.
- Try baby spinach leaves instead of watercress.
- Instead of crème fraîche, use 2 tbsp mayonnaise.

Healthy and sustaining
Cheap eat
Brain food
Comfort food

CHICKEN AND FISH SUPPERS

Nutritional Information (Per Serving)
320 calories, 23g fat (of which 5g saturates), 22g carbohydrate, 0.7g salt
Gluten free · Dairy free · Easy

Serves 4
Preparation time 15 minutes
Cooking time 20 minutes

Food for Friends

Simple Chicken Casserole

4–6 chicken joints
3 tbsp oil
1 onion, peeled and chopped
2 garlic cloves, peeled and crushed
2 celery sticks, chopped
2 carrots, peeled and chopped
1 tbsp plain flour
2 tbsp chopped tarragon or thyme
    or 1 tsp dried
450ml (¾ pint) chicken stock
    (see Top Tips)
salt and ground black pepper

1 Preheat the oven to 180°C (160°C fan oven) mark 4. Cut the chicken legs and breasts in half.

2 Heat the oil in a flameproof casserole and brown the chicken all over. Remove and pour off the excess oil. Add the onion and garlic and brown for a few minutes. Add the vegetables, then stir in the flour and cook for 1 minute. Add the herbs and seasoning, then add the chicken. Pour enough stock into the casserole to come three-quarters of the way up the chicken – you might not need it all, or you might need a little extra water. Cook in the oven for 1–1½ hours.

Top Tips
- If you don't have a flameproof casserole, start everything off in a frying pan, then transfer to the casserole and put in the oven.
- You can use 1 chicken stock cube dissolved in 200ml (7fl oz) boiling water.

Timesaver Tip
Set the alarm on your mobile phone, or use a timer, and let the oven do the work while you get on with other things.

Healthy choice
Comfort food

Serves 4–6
Preparation time 5 minutes
Cooking time 1¼–1½ hours

Nutritional Information (Per Serving)
456 calories, 32g fat (of which 7g saturates), 10g carbohydrate, 1.7g salt
Dairy free · Easy

Lamb Chops
with Crispy Garlic Potatoes

1. Spread the mint sauce over the lamb chops and leave to marinate while you prepare the potatoes.

2. Boil the potatoes in a pan of lightly salted water for 2 minutes until just starting to soften. Drain, tip back into the pan, season and toss through the garlic oil.

3. Meanwhile, heat the olive oil in a large frying pan and fry the chops for 4–5 minutes on each side until just cooked, adding a splash of boiling water to the pan to make a sauce. Remove the chops and sauce from the pan and keep warm.

4. Add the potatoes to the pan. Fry over a medium heat for 10–12 minutes until crisp and golden. Divide the potatoes, chops and sauce among four plates and serve with green beans.

2 tbsp mint sauce (see Top Tip)
8 small lamb chops
3 medium potatoes, peeled and cut into 5mm (¼ in) slices
2 tbsp garlic-flavoured olive oil
1 tbsp olive oil
salt and ground black pepper
steamed green beans to serve

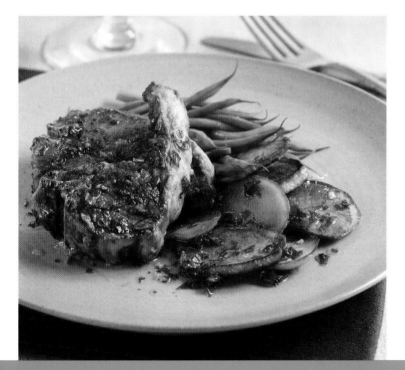

✓ Top Tip
Mint sauce
Finely chop 20g (¾oz) fresh mint and mix with 1 tbsp each olive oil and white wine vinegar.

Ready in under 30 minutes
Quick and easy

Nutritional Information (Per Serving)
835 calories, 45g fat (of which 19g saturates), 22g carbohydrate, 0.7g salt
Gluten free · Dairy free

Serves 4
Preparation time 10 minutes
Cooking time 20 minutes

Pork Chops with Apple Mash

4 large potatoes, peeled and chopped
4 tsp ready-made spice mix
4 pork chops
25g (1oz) butter
knob of butter
1 red apple, cored and chopped
salt

1 Cook the potatoes in a pan of lightly salted water for 10–12 minutes until tender. Meanwhile, rub the spice mix into the pork chops.

2 Heat the butter in a pan. Add the chops and fry for 5 minutes on each side. Remove from the pan and put on warm plates. Add a splash of hot water to the pan and swirl the juices around to make a thin gravy. Drain the potatoes.

3 Melt a knob of butter in another pan. Add the apple and fry for 1–2 minutes until starting to soften. Tip the drained potatoes into the pan, season with salt and pepper and mash roughly with the apple. Serve with the chops and gravy.

Ready in under 30 minutes
Quick and easy
Five ingredients or fewer
Comfort food

Serves 4
Preparation time 5 minutes
Cooking time about 15 minutes

Nutritional Information (Per Serving)
532 calories, 26g fat (of which 11g saturates), 37g carbohydrate, 1.6g salt
Easy

Grilled Garlic Pork

1. Preheat the grill to high. Put the oil into a small bowl, add the garlic and ginger and a pinch of salt and stir well to mix.

2. Grill the pork chops for 7–10 minutes on each side, then remove from the grill. Brush the oil mixture all over the chops, then return to the grill and cook for a further 2 minutes on each side. Serve with stir-fried shredded cabbage.

1 tbsp olive oil
2 garlic cloves, peeled and crushed
5cm (2in) piece fresh root ginger, peeled and grated
4 pork chops
salt
stir-fried shredded cabbage to serve (if you like)

Ready in under 30 minutes
Healthy choice
Five ingredients or fewer
Comfort food

Nutritional Information (Per Serving)
181 calories, 8g fat (of which 2g saturates), 1g carbohydrate, 0.2g salt
Gluten free · Dairy free · Easy

Serves 4
Preparation time 5 minutes
Cooking time 20–25 minutes

Grilled Lamb Steaks
with Mixed Bean Salad

150g (5oz) sunblush tomatoes in oil
1 garlic clove, peeled and crushed
2 rosemary sprigs
4 x 175g (6oz) leg of lamb steaks
½ small red onion, peeled and finely
   sliced
2 x 400g cans mixed beans, drained
   and rinsed
large handful of rocket
salt and ground black pepper

1 Preheat the grill to high. Drain the sunblush tomatoes, reserving the oil. Put the garlic into a large shallow dish with 1 tbsp oil from the tomatoes. Strip the leaves from the rosemary sprigs, snip into small pieces and add to the dish. Season with salt and pepper, then add the lamb and toss to coat.

2 Grill the lamb for 3–4 minutes on each side until cooked but still just pink. Meanwhile, roughly chop the tomatoes and put into a pan with the onion, beans, remaining rosemary, rocket and a further 1 tbsp oil from the tomatoes. Warm through until the rocket starts to wilt. Serve the lamb steaks with the bean salad on warmed plates.

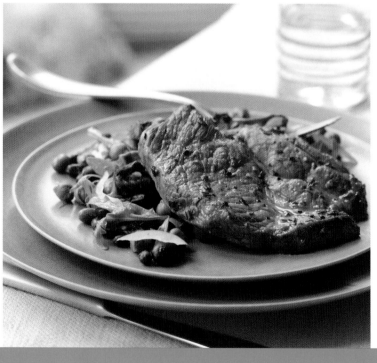

Ready in under 30 minutes
Quick and easy
Healthy and sustaining
Comfort food

Serves 4
Preparation time 5 minutes
Cooking time 10 minutes

Nutritional Information (Per Serving)
545 calories, 20g fat (of which 7g saturates), 30g carbohydrate, 1.8g salt
Gluten free · Dairy free · Easy

One-pot Spicy Beef

1 Heat the oil in a large frying pan. Add the onion to the pan with 2 tbsp water and cook for 10 minutes until softened. Add the garlic and chilli and cook for 1–2 minutes until golden, then add the red peppers and celery and cook for 5 minutes.

2 Add the mince and, as it browns, use a wooden spoon to break up the pieces. Add the tomatoes, beans and Tabasco, then simmer for 20 minutes.

2 tsp sunflower oil
1 large onion, peeled and roughly chopped
1 garlic clove, peeled and finely chopped
1 small red chilli, seeded and finely chopped (see page 50)
2 red peppers, seeded and roughly chopped (see page 50)
2 celery sticks, diced
400g (14oz) minced beef
400g can chopped tomatoes
2 x 400g cans mixed beans, drained and rinsed
1–2 tsp Tabasco

✅ Top Tip

For other recipes using minced meat, see pages 140–1, 151, 222–3, 224.

Healthy and sustaining
Cheap eat
Comfort food

Nutritional Information (Per Serving)
450 calories, 19g fat (of which 7g saturates), 40g carbohydrate, 1.6g salt
Gluten free · Dairy free · Easy

Serves 4
Preparation time 15 minutes
Cooking time about 40 minutes

Cottage Pie

1 tbsp olive oil
1 onion, peeled and finely chopped
2 garlic cloves, peeled and crushed
450g (1lb) minced beef
1 tbsp plain flour
450ml (¾ pint) beef stock (see Top Tip)
2 tbsp Worcestershire sauce
1 medium carrot, peeled and diced
125g (4oz) button mushrooms, sliced
1 kg (2¼ lb) potatoes, mashed
   (see step 3, page 224)
salt and ground black pepper

1 Heat the oil in a large pan, add the onion and fry over a medium heat for 15 minutes until softened and golden, stirring occasionally. Add the garlic and cook for 1 minute.

2 Preheat the oven to 200°C (180°C fan oven) mark 6. Add to the onion and garlic and, as it browns, use a wooden spoon to break up the pieces. Once it's brown, stir in the flour. Stir in the stock to the browned mince, cover the pan with a lid and bring to the boil. Add the Worcestershire sauce, carrot and mushrooms and season well with salt and pepper.

3 Spoon the sauce into a 1.7 litre (3 pint) ovenproof dish, cover with the mashed potato, then cook in the oven for 20–25 minutes.

✔ Top Tip
You can use 1 beef stock cube dissolved in 450ml (¾ pint) boiling water.

★ **Comfort food**

Serves 4
Preparation time 15 minutes
Cooking time 40 minutes

Nutritional Information (Per Serving)
511 calories, 22g fat (of which 8g saturates), 53g carbohydrate, 1.8g salt
Dairy free • Easy

Chilli con Carne

1 Heat the oil in a large pan, add the onion and fry over a medium heat for 15 minutes until softened and golden, stirring occasionally. Add the garlic and cook for 1 minute. Add the red pepper and cook for 5 minutes.

2 Add the mince and, as it browns, use a wooden spoon to break up the pieces. Stir in the chilli powder, stock and tomato purée to the browned mince, cover the pan with a lid and bring to the boil. Add the tomatoes, Worcestershire sauce and mushrooms and season well with salt and pepper. Bring back to the boil, then reduce the heat and simmer, stirring occasionally, for 15 minutes. Add the kidney beans and cook for a further 5 minutes to heat through. Grate some cheese over, if you like, then serve with either rice, jacket potato or tortillas.

1 tbsp olive oil
1 onion, peeled and finely chopped
2 garlic cloves, peeled and crushed
1 red pepper, seeded and chopped (see page 50)
450g (1lb) minced beef
2 tsp chilli powder, mild or hot as you like
300ml (½ pint) beef stock (see Top Tip)
2 tbsp tomato purée
400g can chopped tomatoes
2 tbsp Worcestershire sauce
125g (4oz) button mushrooms, sliced
400g can red kidney beans, rinsed and drained
salt and ground black pepper
grated Cheddar cheese, rice or jacket potatoes or flour tortillas to serve (if you like)

✅ Top Tip

You can use 1 beef stock cube dissolved in 300ml (½ pint) boiling water.

Healthy and sustaining
Cheap eat
Comfort food

FOOD FOR FRIENDS

Nutritional Information (Per Serving)
397 calories, 22g fat (of which 8g saturates), 22g carbohydrate, 2.5g salt
Easy

Serves 4
Preparation time 15 minutes
Cooking time 40 minutes

Shepherd's Pie

1 Heat half the oil in a large pan and brown the mince over a medium to high heat – do this in batches otherwise the meat will steam rather than fry. Remove with a slotted spoon on to a plate.

2 Turn the heat to low and add the remaining oil. Gently fry the onion, mushrooms and carrots for 10 minutes, until softened. Stir in the flour and tomato purée and cook for 1 minute. Return the meat to the pan and add the bay leaf, if you have it. Pour in the stock and bring to the boil, then cover and simmer on a low heat for 25 minutes.

3 Preheat the oven to 200°C (180°C fan) mark 6. Cook the potatoes in lightly salted boiling water for 20 minutes, until tender. Drain and leave to stand in the colander for 2 minutes to steam dry. Melt the butter and milk in the potato pan and add the cooked potatoes. Mash until smooth.

4 Spoon the lamb mixture into a 1.7 litre (3 pint) casserole dish. Remove the bay leaf and check the seasoning. Cover with the mashed potato and sprinkle the cheese over, if you like. Bake for 15–20 minutes, until bubbling and golden. Serve immediately with green vegetables.

2 tbsp sunflower oil
450g (1lb) minced lamb
1 large onion, peeled and chopped
50g (2oz) mushrooms, sliced
2 carrots, peeled and chopped
2 tbsp plain flour
1 tbsp tomato purée
1 bay leaf, if you have it
300ml (½ pint) lamb stock (see Top Tip)
700g (1½lb) potatoes, peeled and cut into large chunks
25g (1oz) butter
60ml (2¼fl oz) milk
50g (2oz) Cheddar cheese, crumbled (if you like)

✓ Top Tip

You can use 1 lamb or vegetable stock cube dissolved in 300ml (½ pint) boiling water.

Healthy and sustaining
Cheap eat
Comfort food

Serves 4
Preparation time 20 minutes
Cooking time about 55 minutes

Nutritional Information (Per Serving)
513 calories, 27g fat (of which 11g saturates), 44g carbohydrate, 0.6g salt
Easy

Beef Stroganoff

1 Cut the steak into strips about 5mm (¼in) wide and 5cm (2in) long.

2 Heat half the butter or oil in a large heavy frying pan over a medium heat. Add the onion and cook gently for 10 minutes or until soft and golden. Remove with a slotted spoon and put to one side. Add the mushrooms to the pan and cook, stirring, for 2–3 minutes until golden brown; remove and put to one side.

3 Increase the heat and add the remaining butter or oil to the pan. Quickly fry the meat, in two or three batches, for 2–3 minutes, stirring constantly to ensure even browning. Remove from the pan. Add the brandy, if using, and allow it to bubble to reduce.

4 Put all the meat, onion and mushrooms back into the pan. Reduce the heat and stir in the mustard, crème fraîche and cream. Heat through, stir in most of the parsley and season with salt and pepper. Serve with rice or noodles, with the remaining parsley scattered over the top.

700g (1½lb) rump or fillet steak, trimmed
50g (2oz) unsalted butter or 4 tbsp olive oil
1 onion, peeled and thinly sliced
225g (8oz) brown-cap mushrooms, sliced
3 tbsp brandy (if you like)
1 tsp French mustard
200ml (7fl oz) crème fraîche
100ml (3½ fl oz) double cream
3 tbsp freshly chopped flat-leafed parsley
salt and ground black pepper
rice or noodles to serve (see pages 61 and 60)

£ Moneysaver Tip

You can omit the crème fraîche and increase the cream to 150ml (¼ pint).

Quick and easy
Comfort food
Great for parties

Nutritional Information (Per Serving)
750 calories, 60g fat (of which 35g saturates), 3g carbohydrate, 0.5g salt
Gluten free · Easy

Serves 4
Preparation time 10 minutes
Cooking time about 20 minutes

Fish and Chips

4 litres (7 pints) sunflower oil for
    deep-frying
125g (4oz) self-raising flour
¼ tsp baking powder
¼ tsp salt
1 medium egg
150ml (¼ pint) sparkling mineral
    water
2 hake fillets, about 125g (4oz) each
450g (1lb) Desirée potatoes, peeled
    and cut into 1cm (½in) chips
salt, vinegar and garlic mayonnaise
    to serve

  1
Heat the oil in a deep-fryer to 190°C (test by frying a small cube
of bread – it should brown in 20 seconds).

  2
Whiz the flour, baking powder, salt, egg and water in a blender
until combined into a batter. (Alternatively, put the ingredients
into a bowl and beat everything together until smooth.) Drop one
of the fish fillets into the batter to coat it.

3
Put half the chips in the deep-fryer, then add the battered fish.
Fry for 6 minutes or until just cooked, then remove and drain
well on kitchen paper. Keep warm if not serving immediately.

4
Drop the remaining fillet into the batter to coat, then repeat
step 3 with the remaining chips. Serve with salt, vinegar and
garlic mayonnaise.

Safety
Deep-frying with hot oil can be
dangerous because the high heat
means it can catch fire:
• Use a pan with a lid.
• Do not wear sleeves that can
  dangle in the oil.
• Do not fill your pan more than
  half full.
• Never put water in hot oil.
• If the oil catches fire, cover with
  the lid, then slide the pan off the
  heat.

Ready in under 30 minutes
Quick and easy
Comfort food

Serves 2
Preparation time 15 minutes
Cooking time 12 minutes

Nutritional Information (Per Serving)
1186 calories, 79g fat (of which 18g saturates), 73g carbohydrate, 3.2g salt
Dairy free • Easy

Pesto Cod with Butter Beans

1 Preheat the grill to medium. Spread each fish fillet evenly with 1 tbsp of the red pesto and grill for 10–15 minutes until the flesh is opaque and just cooked.

2 Meanwhile, heat the oil in a pan and add the butter beans and garlic. Cook for 10 minutes, stirring occasionally and mashing the beans lightly as you do so.

3 Two or three minutes before serving, add the spinach to the pan and allow it to wilt. Spoon the butter beans on to four plates and top with the fish and any juices from grilling. Squeeze a little lemon juice over each piece of fish and serve immediately.

4 small cod or other white fish fillets
4 tbsp red pepper pesto (see Top Tip, page 98)
a generous glug of olive oil
2 x 400g cans butter beans, drained and rinsed
2 garlic cloves, peeled and crushed
225g (8oz) fresh spinach
a squeeze of lemon juice

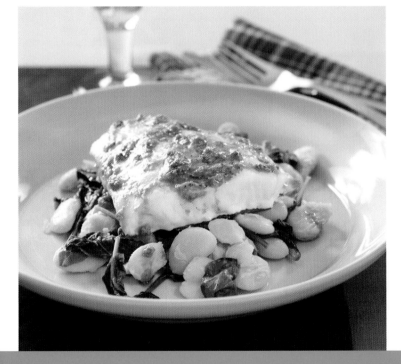

£ Moneysaver Tip

There are lots of alternatives to cod: try pollack, coley or whiting.

Ready in under 30 minutes
Quick and easy
Healthy and sustaining
Brain food

FOOD FOR FRIENDS

Nutritional Information (Per Serving)
403 calories, 16g fat (of which 3g saturates), 24g carbohydrate, 2.5g salt
Gluten free · Easy

Serves 4
Preparation time 5 minutes
Cooking time 15 minutes

Eggs

Courgette and Parmesan
Frittata

40g (1½oz) butter
1 small onion, peeled and finely
    chopped
225g (8oz) courgettes, trimmed and
    finely sliced
6 medium eggs, beaten
25g (1oz) Parmesan, freshly grated,
    plus shavings to garnish
salt and ground black pepper

1 Melt 25g (1oz) butter in a small non-stick frying pan and cook the onion for about 10 minutes until softened. Add the courgettes and fry gently for 5 minutes or until they begin to soften.

2 Beat the eggs in a bowl and season with salt and pepper.

3 Add the remaining butter to the pan and heat, then pour in the eggs. Cook for 2–3 minutes or until golden underneath and cooked around the edges. Meanwhile, preheat the grill to medium.

4 Sprinkle the grated cheese over the frittata and grill for 1–2 minutes until just set – make sure the handle doesn't get too hot. Scatter with Parmesan shavings, cut into quarters and serve with a green salad.

Try Something Different
Cherry Tomato and Rocket Frittata
Replace the courgettes with 175g (6oz) ripe cherry tomatoes, frying them for 1 minute only, until they begin to soften. Immediately after pouring in the eggs, scatter 25g (1oz) rocket leaves over the surface. Continue cooking as in step 3.

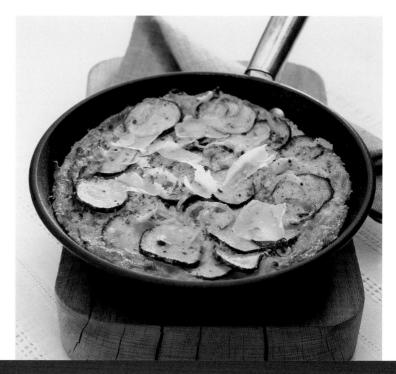

Quick and easy
Five ingredients or fewer
Cheap eat
Brain food

Serves 4
Preparation time 10 minutes
Cooking time 15–20 minutes

Nutritional Information (Per Serving)
229 calories, 19g fat (of which 9g saturates), 2g carbohydrate, 0.6g salt
Gluten free • Easy

Potato and Chorizo
Tortilla

1 Heat the oil in a small non-stick frying pan over a medium-low heat. Add the potatoes, onions and garlic. Stir together until coated in the oil, then cover the pan. Cook gently, stirring occasionally, for 10–15 minutes until the potato is soft. Season with salt, then add the chorizo.

2 Preheat the grill until hot. Season the beaten eggs with salt and pepper and pour over the potato mixture. Cook over a medium heat for 5 minutes or until beginning to brown at the edges and the egg is about three-quarters set. Put the pan under the grill to brown the top – make sure the handle doesn't get too hot. The egg should be a little soft in the middle, as it continues to cook and set as it cools.

3 Carefully loosen the tortilla around the edge and underneath with a knife or spatula. Cut into wedges and serve.

6 tbsp olive oil
450g (1lb) potatoes, peeled and very thinly sliced
225g (8oz) onions, peeled and thinly sliced
2 garlic cloves, peeled and finely chopped
50g (2oz) sliced chorizo, cut into thin strips
6 large eggs, lightly beaten
salt and ground black pepper

Quick and easy
Healthy choice
Cheap eat
Comfort food

EGGS

Nutritional Information (Per Serving)
431 calories, 32g fat (of which 7g saturates), 23g carbohydrate, 0.9g salt
Vegetarian · Dairy free · Easy

Serves 4
Preparation time 5 minutes
Cooking time 25 minutes

231

Poached Eggs
with Mushrooms

8 medium-sized flat mushrooms
40g (1½oz) butter
8 medium eggs
225g (8oz) baby spinach leaves
4 tsp pesto (see Top Tip,
　　page 98)

1 Preheat the oven to 200°C (180°C fan oven) mark 6. Arrange the mushrooms in a single layer in a small roasting tin and dot with the butter. Roast in the oven for 15 minutes until golden brown and soft.

2 Meanwhile, bring a wide shallow pan of water to the boil. When the mushrooms are half-cooked and the water in the pan is bubbling furiously, break the eggs into the pan, spaced well apart, then take the pan off the heat. The eggs will take about 6 minutes to cook.

3 When the mushrooms are tender, put them on a warmed plate, cover and return to the turned-off oven to keep warm.

4 Put the roasting tin over a medium heat on the hob and add the spinach. Cook, stirring, for about 30 seconds until the spinach has just started to wilt.

5 The eggs should be set by now, so divide the mushrooms among four plates and top with a little spinach, a poached egg and a teaspoonful of pesto.

 Moneysaver Tip

Intstead of baby spinach, use sliced spinach leaves.

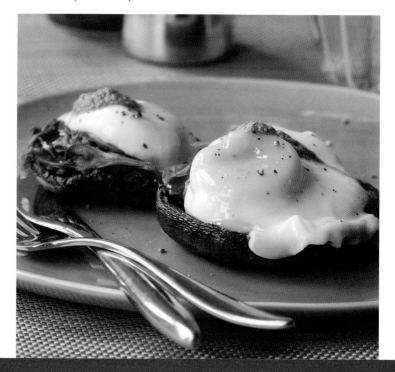

Quick and easy
Healthy choice
Five ingredients or fewer
Cheap eat

Serves 4
Preparation time 15 minutes
Cooking time 20 minutes

Nutritional Information (Per Serving)
276 calories, 23g fat (of which 9g saturates), 1g carbohydrate, 0.7g salt
Vegetarian · Gluten free · Easy

Baked Eggs
with Mushrooms

1. Preheat the oven to 200°C (180°C fan oven) mark 6. Heat the oil in a large frying pan, add the chopped mushrooms and stir-fry for 30 seconds. Add the spinach and stir-fry until wilted. Season to taste, then divide the mixture between two shallow ovenproof dishes.

2. Carefully break an egg into the centre of each dish, then spoon 1 tbsp single cream over each.

3. Cook in the oven for about 12 minutes until just set – the eggs will continue to cook a little once they're out of the oven. Grind a little more pepper over the top, if you like, and serve.

2 tbsp olive oil
125g (4oz) mushrooms, chopped
225g (8oz) fresh spinach
2 medium eggs
2 tbsp single cream
salt and ground black pepper

Ready in under 30 minutes
Quick and easy
Healthy choice
Five ingredients or fewer

EGGS

Nutritional Information (Per Serving)
238 calories, 21g fat (of which 5g saturates), 2g carbohydrate, 0.6g salt
Vegetarian · Gluten free · Easy

Serves 2
Preparation time 10 minutes
Cooking time 15 minutes

Chorizo Hash

1 Preheat the oven to 200°C (180°C fan oven) mark 6. Cook the potatoes in lightly salted boiling water for 15–20 minutes until just tender. Drain well, then return to the pan and cover with a lid to keep them warm and dry off any moisture.

2 While the potatoes are cooking, cut the sausage into small dice, then fry in a roasting tin – no need to add any fat – over a high heat until it has turned a deep golden brown and is beginning to go crispy at the edges – about 15 minutes.

3 Remove the sausage from the tin with a fork or slotted spoon on to a plate and put to one side. Add the chopped onion to the tin and fry over a medium heat for a good 10 minutes until it turns golden brown. There should be enough oil from the sausage without having to add any extra oil.

4 Cut the cooked potatoes into smaller dice. Return the sausage and potatoes to the tin and cook over a medium heat for 5 minutes, without stirring, until a golden crust forms on the bottom of the mixture. Break up the mixture, then cook again until another crust forms. Break up the mixture again and leave to cook for 2–3 minutes more.

5 Make four dips in the potato cake and crack an egg into each one. Cook in the oven for about 7 minutes or until the egg whites are set but the yolks are still soft. Season the eggs with salt and serve at once.

700g (1½lb) large floury potatoes, peeled and cut into large chunks
175g (6oz) chorizo sausage, in one piece, rind peeled off and discarded
1 large onion, peeled and finely chopped
4 medium eggs
salt

Five ingredients or fewer
Cheap eat
Brain food
Comfort food

Serves 4
Preparation time 10 minutes
Cooking time 35–45 minutes

Nutritional Information (Per Serving)
358 calories, 17g fat (of which 6g saturates), 34g carbohydrate, 0.9g salt
Easy

Creamy Baked Eggs

 Preheat the oven to 180°C (160°C fan oven) mark 4. Grease four individual ramekins.

 Put 1 tomato in each ramekin and season with salt and pepper. Carefully break an egg on top of each, then drizzle 1 tbsp cream over each egg.

3 Bake for 15–18 minutes – the eggs will continue to cook once they have been taken out of the oven.

4 Leave to stand for 2 minutes before serving. Serve with bread.

oil to grease
4 sun-dried tomatoes
4 medium eggs
4 tbsp double cream
salt and ground black pepper
bread to serve (Granary is good)

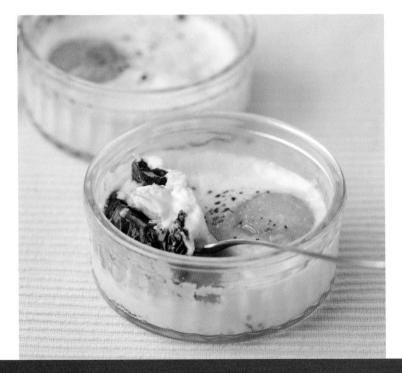

Quick and easy
Five ingredients or fewer
Cheap eat
Brain food

EGGS

Nutritional Information (Per Serving)
153 calories, 14g fat (of which 7g saturates), 1g carbohydrate, 0.2g salt
Vegetarian • Gluten free • Easy

Serves 4
Preparation time 5 minutes
Cooking time 15–18 minutes

235

Veggies

Baked Jacket Potatoes

Posh Jacket Potatoes

Bubble and Squeak Cakes

Buttered Cabbage

Green Beans and Flaked Almonds

Warm Broad Bean and Feta Salad

Roasted Mediterranean Vegetables

Charred Courgettes

Roasted Vegetable Salad

Spinach with Tomatoes

Baked Jacket Potatoes

6 large baking potatoes, scrubbed
50–75g (2–3oz) butter
salt and pepper

 1 Preheat the oven to 200°C (180°C fan oven) mark 6. Scrub the potatoes and prick all over with a fork. Put them on a baking sheet and bake in the oven for 1½ hours or until the potatoes feel soft when gently squeezed, turning them over once.

2 When the potatoes are cooked, score a deep cross on each one, season with salt and pepper and top with a generous knob of butter to serve.

00:00 Timesaver Tip
Set the alarm on your mobile phone, or use a timer, and let the oven do the work while you get on with other things.

Try Something Different
Top the jacket potatoes with grated cheese, or crème fraîche and chopped chives, or soured cream and chopped spring onions.

Healthy and sustaining
Five ingredients or fewer
Cheap eat
Comfort food

Serves 6
Preparation time 5 minutes
Cooking time about 1½ hours

Nutritional Information (Per Serving)
265 calories, 9g fat (of which 5g saturates), 43g carbohydrate, 0.8g salt
Gluten free · Vegetarian · Easy

Posh Jacket Potatoes

1 Preheat the oven to 200°C (180°C fan oven) mark 6. Prick the potato skins all over with a fork, rub with oil and sprinkle with salt. Cook in the oven for 1 hour. Twenty minutes before the end of the cooking time, put the garlic cloves into a small roasting tin and cook for 20 minutes.

2 Squeeze the potatoes gently to check they are well cooked, then remove the potatoes and garlic from the oven and leave to cool slightly. When cool enough to handle, slice the tops off the potatoes and scoop the flesh into a warm bowl. Squeeze the garlic out of its skin and add it to the potato flesh with the butter, crème fraîche and mustard seeds. Season to taste with salt and pepper, then mash well. Return the potato mixture to the hollowed skins.

3 Put the filled potatoes on a baking sheet, or into a baking tin, and return to the oven for 15 minutes or until golden brown. Garnish with oregano sprigs, if you like, and serve hot.

6 large baking potatoes, scrubbed
2 tbsp sunflower oil
1 tbsp coarse sea salt
4–5 large garlic cloves, unpeeled
50g (2oz) butter
6 tbsp crème fraîche
2 tbsp mustard seeds, toasted and lightly crushed
salt and ground black pepper
fresh oregano sprigs to garnish (if you like)

00:00 Timesaver Tip

Set the alarm on your mobile phone, or use a timer, and let the oven do the work while you get on with other things.

Cheap eat
Comfort food
Share with friends

VEGGIES

Nutritional Information (Per Serving)
315 calories, 17g fat (of which 9g saturates), 38g carbohydrate, 1g salt
Vegetarian • Gluten free • Easy

Serves 6
Preparation time 15–20 minutes
Cooking time 1¼ hours

Bubble and Squeak Cakes

550g (1¼lb) old potatoes, peeled
125g (4oz) butter
175g (6oz) leeks, trimmed and finely
  shredded
175g (6oz) green cabbage, finely
  shredded
plain flour to dust
1 tbsp oil
salt and ground black pepper

1 Cook the potatoes in a large pan of lightly salted boiling water for about 20 minutes until tender, then drain and mash.

2 Heat 50g (2oz) butter in a large non-stick frying pan. Add the leeks and cabbage and fry for 5 minutes, stirring, or until soft and beginning to colour. Combine the leeks and cabbage with the potatoes and season well with salt and pepper. Leave to cool. When cool enough to handle, mould into 12 cakes and dust with flour.

3 Heat the oil and remaining butter in a non-stick frying pan and cook the cakes for 4 minutes on each side or until they are golden, crisp and hot right through. Serve.

**Cheap eat
Comfort food**

VEGGIES

Makes 12
Preparation time 15 minutes
Cooking time 45 minutes, plus cooling

Nutritional Information (Per Cake)
130 calories, 10g fat (of which 6g saturates), 10g carbohydrate, 0.2g salt
Vegetarian · Easy

Buttered Cabbage

1 Cook the cabbage in lightly salted boiling water until just tender. Drain well.

2 Meanwhile, fry the caraway seeds, if you have them, in a dry pan until toasted. Take the pan off the heat, add the butter and leave to melt in the heat of the pan.

3 Toss the butter through the cabbage and serve with a squeeze of lemon juice.

450g (1lb) finely shredded cabbage
½ tsp caraway seeds (optional)
50g (2oz) butter
juice of ½ lemon

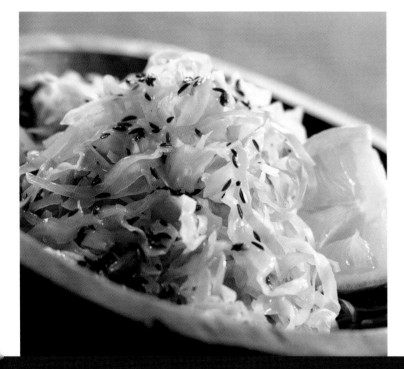

Ready in under 30 minutes
Quick and easy
Healthy choice
Five ingredients or fewer

VEGGIES

Nutritional Information (Per Serving)
122 calories, 11g fat (of which 7g saturates), 4g carbohydrate, 0.2g salt
Vegetarian • Gluten free • Easy

Serves 4
Preparation time 5 minutes
Cooking time about 10 minutes

Green Beans
and Flaked Almonds

200g (7oz) green beans
1 tsp olive oil
25g (1oz) flaked almonds
½ lemon

 Bring a large pan of water to the boil. Add the green beans and cook for 4–5 minutes. Drain.

 Meanwhile, heat the oil in a large frying pan. Add the almonds and cook for 1–2 minutes until golden. Turn off the heat, add the drained beans to the frying pan and toss. Squeeze over a little lemon juice just before serving.

Try Something Different
Use pinenuts instead of almonds, drizzle with balsamic vinegar and scatter with basil leaves to serve.

Buttery Runner Beans
Cook the beans as above, then drain well. Add a knob of butter and season well. Toss together and serve.

Quick and easy
Healthy choice
Five ingredients or fewer

VEGGIES

242

Serves 4
Preparation time 5 minutes
Cooking time 5–7 minutes

Nutritional Information (Per Serving)
57 calories, 5g fat (of which trace saturates), 2g carbohydrate, 0g salt
Vegetarian • Gluten free • Dairy free • Easy

Warm Broad Bean
and Feta Salad

1 Cook the beans in lightly salted boiling water for 3–5 minutes until tender. Drain, then plunge into cold water and drain again.

2 Tip the beans into a bowl, add the feta cheese, mint, olive oil and a squeeze of lemon juice. Season well with salt and pepper and toss together. Serve with lemon wedges, if you like.

225g (8oz) frozen broad beans
100g (3½ oz) feta cheese, chopped
2 tbsp freshly chopped mint
2 tbsp extra virgin olive oil
a squeeze of lemon juice
salt and ground black pepper
lemon wedges to serve (if you like)

Ready in under **30 minutes**
Quick and easy
Healthy choice
Five ingredients or fewer

VEGGIES

Nutritional Information (Per Serving)
321 calories, 22g fat (of which 8g saturates), 15g carbohydrate, 1.8g salt
Vegetarian · Gluten free · Easy

Serves 2
Preparation time 10 minutes
Cooking time 5 minutes

Roasted Mediterranean
Vegetables

4 tomatoes, halved
2 onions, peeled and quartered
4 red peppers, seeded and cut into
   strips (see page 50)
2 courgettes, trimmed and cut into
   thick slices
4 garlic cloves, unpeeled
6 tbsp olive oil
1 tbsp freshly chopped thyme leaves
salt and ground black pepper

1 Preheat the oven to 220°C (200°C fan oven) mark 7. Put the tomatoes into a large roasting tin with the onions, peppers, courgettes and garlic. Drizzle with the oil and sprinkle with thyme, salt and pepper.

2 Roast in the oven, turning occasionally, for 35–40 minutes until tender.

Swap
- Sprinkle with toasted sesame seeds and serve with hummus.
- Use oregano instead of thyme.

Healthy choice
Cheap eat
Comfort food
Share with friends

VEGGIES

Serves 4
Preparation time 10 minutes
Cooking time 35–40 minutes

Nutritional Information (Per Serving)
252 calories, 18g fat (of which 3g saturates), 19g carbohydrate, 0.4g salt
Vegetarian · Gluten free · Dairy free · Easy

Charred Courgettes

1 Preheat the grill or barbecue, or use a griddle pan. Score a criss-cross pattern on the fleshy side of the courgettes. Brush lightly with olive oil and sprinkle with salt.

2 Cook the courgettes for 10 minutes or until just tender, turning them occasionally.

4 courgettes, halved lengthways
olive oil to brush
salt to sprinkle

 Swap

- Mix the olive oil with a good pinch of dried chilli flakes and a small handful of chopped fresh rosemary leaves.
- Use a mixture of yellow and green courgettes, if you like.

Ready in under 30 minutes
Quick and easy
Healthy choice
Five ingredients or fewer

VEGGIES

Nutritional Information (Per Serving)
36 calories, 2g fat (of which trace saturates), 2g carbohydrate, 0g salt
Vegetarian · Gluten free · Dairy free · Easy

Serves 4
Preparation time 5 minutes
Cooking time 10 minutes

Roasted Vegetable Salad

900g (2lb) mixed vegetables, such
   as fennel, courgettes, leeks,
   aubergines, baby turnips, new
   potatoes and red onions
2 garlic cloves, unpeeled
4–5 fresh marjoram or rosemary
   sprigs
5 tbsp olive oil
1 tsp flaked sea salt
mixed crushed peppercorns to taste
4 tsp balsamic vinegar
warm crusty bread to serve

**FOR THE MUSTARD
   MAYONNAISE**
150ml (¼ pint) mayonnaise
2 tbsp Dijon mustard
salt and ground black pepper

1 Preheat the oven to 220°C (200°C fan oven) mark 7. For the
vegetables, quarter the fennel, chop the courgettes, leeks and
aubergines and peel the turnips and onions, then cut the onions
into wedges. Place the vegetables, garlic, marjoram or rosemary,
the oil, salt and peppercorns in a roasting tin and toss well (see
Top Tip).

2 Cook in the oven for 30–35 minutes or until the vegetables are
golden, tossing frequently. Sprinkle the vinegar over them and
return to the oven for a further 5 minutes.

3 To make the mustard mayonnaise, mix together the mayonnaise
and mustard, then season with salt and pepper and set aside.

4 Arrange the vegetable salad on a serving dish and serve with
crusty bread.

 Top Tip
It's best to roast vegetables in a
single layer or they will steam
and become soggy. Use two tins
if necessary.

 Quick and easy
Healthy choice
Cheap eat

VEGGIES

Serves 4
Preparation time 15 minutes
Cooking time 40 minutes

Nutritional Information (Per Serving)
420 calories, 43g fat (of which 6g saturates), 5g carbohydrate, 1g salt
Vegetarian · Gluten free · Dairy free · Easy

Spinach with Tomatoes

1 Heat half the butter in a pan, add the garlic and cook until just soft. Add the tomatoes and cook for 4–5 minutes until just beginning to soften.

2 Put the spinach and a little water in a clean pan, cover and cook for 2–3 minutes until just wilted. Drain well, chop roughly and stir into the tomatoes.

3 Add the remaining butter and heat through gently. Season well with salt and pepper, stir in the nutmeg and serve.

50g (2oz) butter
2 garlic cloves, peeled and crushed
450g (1lb) tomatoes, halved (baby plum tomatoes are good for this)
250g (9oz) baby spinach leaves
a large pinch of freshly grated nutmeg
salt and ground black pepper

✅ Top Tip
Instead of baby spinach leaves, use shredded spinach.

Ready in under 30 minutes
Quick and easy
Healthy choice
Five ingredients or fewer

VEGGIES

Nutritional Information (Per Serving)
85 calories, 7g fat (of which 5g saturates), 3g carbohydrate, 0.3g salt
Vegetarian · Gluten free · Easy

Serves 6
Preparation time 10 minutes
Cooking time 15 minutes

247

Meat-free Meals

Getting the Balance Right

If you're a vegetarian or vegan, as with any diet, variety is all important. Provided a vegetarian diet includes a good range of cereals and grains, pulses, nuts and seeds, fruit and vegetables, dairy and/or soya products, it should be nutritionally sound. A small quantity of plant oils, margarine or butter is needed to provide essential fatty acids and vitamins.

SOURCES OF PROTEIN

Most vegetarians needn't worry about getting enough protein: this nutrient is found in a wide variety of foods, including pulses, tofu and other soya bean products, Quorn, eggs, cheese, sprouted beans, nuts and seeds.

MEAT SUBSTITUTES

PULSES
These are all the various beans, peas and lentils. They are highly nutritious, especially when eaten with grains, such as couscous, pasta, rice or bread. Canned pulses are a convenient, quick alternative to soaking and cooking dried ones and most supermarkets stock a wide range. A 400g can (drained weight about 235g) is roughly equivalent to 100g (3½oz) dried beans. The dried beans double in weight after soaking.

SPROUTED BEANS AND SEEDS
These are rich in nutrients and lend a nutty taste and crunchy texture to salads and stir-fries. Fresh bean sprouts are available from most supermarkets.

VEGETARIAN CHEESES
Most supermarkets and cheese shops now stock a range of vegetarian cheeses, produced using vegetarian rennet. See page 37.

TOFU

Also known as bean curd, tofu is made from ground soya beans. It is highly nutritious but virtually tasteless. However, it readily absorbs other flavours when marinated. It is available as firm, silken and smoked.

Tofu is sold as a chilled product and should be stored in the fridge. Once the packet is opened, the tofu should be kept immersed in a bowl of water in the fridge and eaten within four days.

TEXTURED VEGETABLE PROTEIN (TVP)
This forms the bulk of most ready-prepared vegetarian burgers, sausages and mince. It is made from a mixture of soya flour, flavourings and liquid. It has a slightly chewy, meat-like texture. TVP can be included in stews, pies, curries and other dishes, rather as meat would be used by non-vegetarians.

QUORN
The vegetarian product, Quorn, is derived from a distant relative of the mushroom and is a good source of complete protein for vegetarians. Like tofu, Quorn has a bland flavour and benefits from being marinated before cooking. Available from the chiller cabinet, Quorn should be kept in the fridge.

Quick Winter Minestrone

1. Heat the oil in a large pan and add the onion, carrot and celery. Cook for 8–10 minutes until softened, then add the garlic and thyme and fry for another 2–3 minutes.

2. Add the hot stock, tomatoes and half the borlotti beans. Mash the remaining beans, stir into the soup and simmer for 30 minutes, adding the minestrone pasta and cabbage for the last 10 minutes of cooking time.

3. Check the seasoning, then serve the soup in individual bowls with a dollop of pesto on top and slices of toasted ciabatta drizzled with extra virgin olive oil on the side, if you like.

2 tbsp olive oil
1 small onion, peeled and finely chopped
1 carrot, peeled and chopped
1 celery stick, chopped
1 garlic clove, peeled and crushed
2 tbsp chopped fresh thyme
1 litre (1¾ pints) hot vegetable stock (see Top Tip)
400g can chopped tomatoes
400g can borlotti beans, drained and rinsed
125g (4oz) minestrone pasta
175g (6oz) Savoy cabbage, shredded
salt and ground black pepper
pesto (see Top Tip, page 98), toasted ciabatta and extra virgin olive oil to serve (if you like)

Top Tip
You can use 2 stock cubes dissolved in 1 litre (1¾ pints) boiling water.

Healthy and sustaining
Cheap eat
Comfort food
Share with friends

Nutritional Information (Per Serving)
334 calories, 11g fat (of which 3g saturates), 47g carbohydrate, 1.5g salt
Vegetarian • Easy

Serves 4
Preparation time 10 minutes
Cooking time 45 minutes

Leek and Potato Pie

2 medium potatoes, peeled and
    chopped
1 large leek, chopped
butter
25g (1oz) grated Cheddar cheese
salt and ground black pepper

 Put the potatoes into a pan of lightly salted water, cover and bring to the boil. Simmer for 10–15 minutes until tender.

 Meanwhile, heat a little butter in a frying pan. Add the leek and fry for 10–15 minutes until soft and golden. Preheat the grill.

3 Drain the potatoes and tip back into the pan. Season with salt and pepper, then mash with a small knob of butter. Put the leek into a small, ovenproof dish and cover with the mash. Top the pie with the cheese, then cook under the hot grill for 10 minutes or until hot and golden.

MEAT-FREE MEALS

Healthy choice
Five ingredients or fewer
Cheap eat
Comfort food

Serves 1
Preparation time 5 minutes
Cooking time 25 minutes

Nutritional Information (Per Serving)
474 calories, 22g fat (of which 13g saturates), 56g carbohydrate, 0.7g salt
Vegetarian • Gluten free • Easy

Potato and Onion Pan Fry

1 Put the potatoes into a pan of lightly salted boiling water and boil for 2–3 minutes. Meanwhile, heat the oil in a pan and fry the onion for 5 minutes. Drain the potatoes and add to the pan.

2 Cook for 5–10 minutes until golden and crisp, then season well and toss through the parsley to serve.

500g (1lb 2oz) potatoes, peeled and thickly sliced
2–3 tbsp olive oil
1 onion, peeled and cut into 8 wedges
1 tbsp freshly chopped flat-leafed parsley
salt and ground black pepper

✅ **Top Tip**
To make this dish into a complete meal, serve with fried or hardboiled eggs, baked beans or red kidney beans in chilli sauce.

Ready in under 30 minutes
Quick and easy
Five ingredients or fewer
Cheap eat

MEAT-FREE MEALS

Nutritional Information (Per Serving)
157 calories, 6g fat (of which 1g saturates), 24g carbohydrate, 0.6g salt
Vegetarian · Gluten free · Dairy free · Easy

Serves 4
Preparation time 5 minutes
Cooking time 10–15 minutes

Cauliflower Cheese

1 cauliflower
1 quantity cheese sauce
   (see page 29)
extra grated cheese to sprinkle
salt

1 Preheat the grill. Remove the coarse outer leaves from the cauliflower, cut a cross in the stalk end and give the whole cauliflower a good wash under the tap.

2 Put the cauliflower into a medium pan, with the stem side down, then pour over enough boiling water to come halfway up it. Add a pinch of salt and cover the pan. Bring to the boil and cook for 10–15 minutes. Stick a sharp knife into the florets – they should be tender but not mushy.

3 Drain the cauliflower and put it into an ovenproof dish. Pour the cheese sauce over it, sprinkle with a little grated cheese, then grill for 2–3 minutes until golden on top. Serve on its own or with a jacket potato.

Try Something Different

Make this with ½ head of cauliflower and ½ head of broccoli. Cut the stems off the florets, then peel and chop them into pieces the same size as the cauliflower and broccoli florets. They will take only about 4 minutes to cook until just tender. Make as above.

Quick and easy
Healthy choice
Five ingredients or fewer
Cheap eat

Serves 2
Preparation time 5 minutes
Cooking time 20 minutes

Nutritional Information (Per Serving)
383 calories, 24g fat (of which 14g saturates), 20g carbohydrate, 2.2g salt
Vegetarian • Easy

Rice-stuffed Peppers

1 Preheat the oven to 200°C (180°C fan oven) mark 6. Cook the rice according to the pack instructions, then drain.

2 Meanwhile, heat the oil in a pan, add the onions and fry for 15 minutes. Add the tomatoes and leave to simmer for 10 minutes. Stir in the cooked rice, then spoon the mixture into the halved peppers.

3 Put the peppers into a roasting tin and pour the stock around them. Cook in the oven for 30 minutes until tender. Serve sprinkled with coriander sprigs, if you like.

225g (8oz) brown rice
1 tbsp olive oil
2 onions, peeled and chopped
400g can tomatoes (cherry tomatoes are good for this)
3 tbsp freshly chopped coriander, plus extra sprigs to garnish (if you like)
4 red peppers, halved and seeded, leaving stalks intact (see page 50)
150ml (¼ pint) hot vegetable stock (see Top Tips)

✅ Top Tips

- You can use ½ vegetable stock cube dissolved in 150ml (¼ pint) boiling water.
- To make the dish into a complete meal add 50g (2oz) chopped blanched almonds or chopped cashew nuts to the cooked rice and coriander at step 2.

**Healthy choice
Cheap eat**

MEAT-FREE MEALS

Nutritional Information (Per Serving)
208 calories, 5g fat (of which 1g saturates), 39g carbohydrate, 0g salt
Vegetarian • Gluten free • Dairy free • Easy

Preparation time 15 minutes
Cooking time 55 minutes
Serves 4

Peppers Stuffed
with Mushrooms

40g (1½oz) butter

4 red peppers, halved and seeded, leaving the stalks intact (see page 50)

3 tbsp olive oil

350g (12oz) chestnut mushrooms, roughly chopped

4 tbsp freshly chopped chives

100g (3½oz) feta cheese (see pages 37 and 250)

50g (2oz) fresh white breadcrumbs (see step 1, page 131)

25g (1oz) freshly grated Parmesan (see pages 37 and 250)

salt and ground black pepper

1 Preheat the oven to 180°C (160°C fan oven) mark 4. Use a little of the butter to grease a shallow ovenproof dish, then put in the peppers side by side, hollow side up.

2 Heat the remaining butter and 1 tbsp of the oil in a pan. Add the mushrooms and fry until they are golden and there's no excess liquid left in the pan. Stir in the chives, then spoon the mixture into the pepper halves.

3 Crumble the feta cheese over the mushrooms. Mix the breadcrumbs and Parmesan in a bowl, then sprinkle the mixture over the top.

4 Season with salt and pepper and drizzle with the remaining oil. Roast for 45 minutes or until golden and tender. Serve warm.

Healthy choice
Cheap eat
Comfort food
Share with friends

Serves 4
Preparation time 20 minutes
Cooking time about 50 minutes

Nutritional Information (Per Serving)
375 calories, 25g fat (of which 11g saturates), 27g carbohydrate, 1.5g salt
Vegetarian • Easy

Mushrooms Stuffed
with Couscous

1 Preheat the oven to 220°C (200°C fan oven) mark 7. Put the couscous into a bowl with the boiling water, the parsley, antipasti and 1 tbsp of the reserved oil. Stir well.

2 Put the mushrooms on a greased baking tray and spoon a little of the couscous mixture into the centre of each. Cook in the oven while you make the sauce.

3 Meanwhile, whisk together the butter, flour and milk in a small pan over a high heat until the mixture comes to the boil. Reduce the heat as soon as it starts to thicken, then whisk constantly until smooth. Take the pan off the heat and stir in the cheese.

4 Spoon the sauce over the mushrooms and sprinkle with the remaining cheese. Put back into the oven for a further 7–10 minutes until golden. Serve with a green salad.

125g (4oz) couscous (see Top Tip)
200ml (7fl oz) boiling water
20g pack fresh flat-leafed parsley, roughly chopped
280g jar mixed antipasti in oil, drained and oil put to one side
8 large flat mushrooms
25g (1oz) butter
25g (1oz) plain flour
300ml (½ pint) skimmed milk
75g (3oz) mature Cheddar cheese, grated, plus extra to sprinkle (see pages 37 and 250)
green salad to serve

✓ Top Tip
Couscous
Often mistaken for a grain, couscous is actually a type of pasta that originated in North Africa. It is perfect for serving with stews and casseroles, or making into salads. The tiny pellets do not require cooking and can simply be soaked. Measure the couscous in a jug and add 1½ times the volume of hot water or stock. Cover the bowl and leave to soak for 5 minutes. Fluff up with a fork before serving. If using for a salad, leave the couscous to cool completely before adding the other salad ingredients.

Ready in under 30 minutes
Quick and easy
Healthy choice
Cheap eat

MEAT-FREE MEALS

Nutritional Information (Per Serving)
340 calories, 21g fat (of which 9g saturates), 26g carbohydrate, 0.6g salt
Vegetarian · Easy

Serves 4
Preparation time 3 minutes
Cooking time about 12 minutes

257

Cheese and Vegetable Bake

250g (9oz) macaroni
1 cauliflower, cut into florets
   (see page 52)
2 leeks, finely chopped
100g (3½ oz) frozen peas
25g (1oz) wholemeal breadcrumbs
   (see step 1, page 131)
crusty bread to serve

FOR THE CHEESE SAUCE
15g (½ oz) butter
15g (½ oz) plain flour
200ml (7fl oz) skimmed milk
75g (3oz) freshly grated Parmesan
   (see Top Tip)
2 tsp Dijon mustard
salt and ground black pepper

1 Cook the macaroni in a large pan of boiling water for 6 minutes, adding the cauliflower and leeks for the last 4 minutes and the peas for the last 2 minutes.

2 Meanwhile, make the cheese sauce. Melt the butter in a pan and add the flour. Cook for 1–2 minutes, then take off the heat and gradually stir in the milk. Bring to the boil slowly, stirring until the sauce thickens. Stir in 50g (2oz) Parmesan and the mustard. Season to taste with salt and pepper.

3 Preheat the grill to medium. Drain the pasta and the vegetables and put back in the pan. Add the cheese sauce and mix well. Spoon into a large shallow 2 litre (3½ pint) ovenproof dish and scatter the remaining Parmesan and the breadcrumbs over. Grill for 5 minutes or until golden and crisp. Serve hot with bread.

✔ Top Tip
A wide range of vegetarian cheeses is available, see page 37.

Quick and easy
Healthy choice
Cheap eat
Comfort food

Serves 4
Preparation time 15 minutes
Cooking time 15 minutes

Nutritional Information (Per Serving)
471 calories, 13g fat (of which 7g saturates), 67g carbohydrate, 0.8g salt
Vegetarian · Easy

Roasted Ratatouille

1 Preheat the oven to 240°C (220°C fan oven) mark 9. Put the peppers, aubergine, onions, garlic, oil and fennel seeds, if using, into a roasting tin. Season with salt and pepper and toss together.

2 Put into the oven and cook for 30 minutes (tossing frequently during cooking) or until the vegetables are charred and beginning to soften.

3 Using oven gloves, carefully remove the tin from the oven. Stir the passata through the vegetables, then put the roasting tin back in the oven for another 50–60 minutes, stirring occasionally. Garnish with the thyme sprigs, if you like, and serve.

400g (14oz) red peppers, seeded and roughly chopped (see page 50)
700g (1½lb) aubergines, stalk removed, cut into chunks
450g (1lb) onions, peeled and cut into wedges
4 or 5 garlic cloves, unpeeled and left whole
150ml (¼ pint) olive oil
1 tsp fennel seeds (if you like)
200ml (7fl oz) passata sauce (puréed and sieved tomatoes, available in jars)
salt and ground black pepper
a few fresh thyme sprigs to garnish (if you like)

£ Moneysaver Tip
Instead of passata, blend 200g (7oz) canned tomatoes.

✔ Top Tip
To make the dish into a complete meal stir in 2 ×160g packs of smoked or marinated tofu chunks after 30 minutes of cooking time.

Timesaver Tip
Set the alarm on your mobile phone, or use a timer, and let the oven do the work while you get on with other things.

MEAT-FREE MEALS

Nutritional Information (Per Serving)
224 calories, 18g fat (of which 3g saturates), 14g carbohydrate, 0.4g salt
Vegetarian · Gluten free · Dairy free · Easy

Serves 6
Preparation time 15 minutes
Cooking time 1½ hours

259

Grilled Sweet Potatoes
with Feta and Olives

1 large sweet potato, weighing about
   500g (1lb 2oz)
4 tbsp olive oil, plus extra to brush
200g (7oz) feta cheese
2 tsp dried mixed herbs
50g (2oz) pitted black olives, chopped
1 garlic clove, peeled and crushed
salt and ground black pepper
flat-leafed parsley sprigs to garnish
   (if you like)

1 Preheat the barbecue or grill. Peel the sweet potato and cut lengthways into eight wedges. Put them into a pan of boiling water and bring back to the boil, then reduce the heat and simmer for 3 minutes. Drain and put in cold water. Drain again, dry well on kitchen paper, then brush lightly with olive oil. Season with salt and pepper, then barbecue or grill for 10–15 minutes until well browned and cooked through.

2 Meanwhile, mash the cheese, herbs, olives, garlic and 4 tbsp olive oil together. Serve the sweet potato with the feta cheese mixture, garnished with flat-leafed parsley, if you like.

Healthy choice
Cheap eat
Comfort food
Share with friends

Serves 4
Preparation time 15 minutes
Cooking time 15–20 minutes

Nutritional Information (Per Serving)
324 calories, 23g fat (of which 9g saturates), 21g carbohydrate, 2.5g salt
Vegetarian · Gluten free · Easy

Thai Vegetable Curry

1 Put the curry paste into a large pan. Add the ginger to the pan with the cashew nuts. Stir over a medium heat for 2–3 minutes.

2 Add the coconut milk, cover and bring to the boil. Stir the carrots into the pan and simmer for 5 minutes, then add the broccoli florets and simmer for a further 5 minutes or until the vegetables are tender.

3 Stir the coriander and lime zest into the pan with the spinach. Squeeze the lime juice over and serve with basmati rice.

2–3 tbsp Thai red curry paste (see Top Tip)
2.5cm (1in) piece fresh root ginger, peeled and finely chopped
50g (2oz) cashew nuts
400ml can coconut milk
3 carrots, cut into thin batons
1 broccoli head, cut into florets (see page 52)
20g (¾oz) fresh coriander, roughly chopped
zest and juice of 1 lime
2 large handfuls of washed spinach leaves
basmati rice to serve

✅ Top Tip
Not all curry pastes are vegetarian, so check the label.

Healthy choice
Cheap eat
Comfort food
Share with friends

MEAT-FREE MEALS

Nutritional Information (Per Serving)
203 calories, 12g fat (of which 2g saturates), 16g carbohydrate, 0.6g salt
Vegetarian · Easy

Serves 4
Preparation time 15 minutes
Cooking time 15 minutes

Chilli Onions with Goat's Cheese

75g (3oz) unsalted butter, softened
2 medium red chillies, seeded and
   finely chopped (see page 50)
1 tsp dried chilli flakes
6 small red onions, peeled
3 x 100g (3½oz) goat's cheese logs,
   with rind
salt and ground black pepper
balsamic vinegar to serve

1 Preheat the oven to 200°C (180°C fan oven) mark 6. Put the butter in a small bowl, beat in the fresh and dried chillies and season well with salt and pepper.

2 Cut off the root from one of the onions, sit it on its base, then make several deep cuts in the top to create a star shape, slicing about two-thirds of the way down the onion. Do the same with the other five onions, then divide the chilli butter equally among them, pushing it down into the cuts.

3 Put the onions in a small roasting tin, cover with foil and bake for 40–45 minutes until soft. About 5 minutes before they are ready, slice each goat's cheese in two, leaving the rind intact, then put on a baking sheet and bake for 2–3 minutes. To serve, put each onion on top of a piece of goat's cheese and drizzle with balsamic vinegar.

Share with friends
Great for parties

MEAT-FREE MEALS

Serves 6
Preparation time 15 minutes
Cooking time 45 minutes

Nutritional Information (Per Serving)
276 calories, 23g fat (of which 16g saturates), 5g carbohydrate, 0.9g salt
Vegetarian · Gluten free · Easy

Potato and Broccoli Curry

1 Cook the potatoes in a pan of lightly salted boiling water for 5 minutes, then drain.

2 Meanwhile, stir the spice mix ingredients together with a good pinch of salt. Dry-fry the spice mix for 2–3 minutes in a large frying pan, then add the oil and onions and fry for 7–8 minutes until soft and golden.

3 Add the potatoes, chickpeas and hot stock. Season to taste with salt and pepper, then cook for 15–20 minutes, adding the broccoli for the last 4–5 minutes of cooking time. Serve with the mango chutney, yogurt and naan bread.

600g (1lb 5oz) new potatoes, scrubbed and cut into bite-size cubes
2 tbsp sunflower oil
2 onions, peeled and sliced
400g can chickpeas, drained and rinsed
250ml (9fl oz) hot vegetable stock (see Top Tips)
150g (5oz) chopped broccoli (see page 52)
salt and ground black pepper
2 tbsp each mango chutney and Greek yogurt, mixed together, and naan bread to serve

FOR THE SPICE MIX
2 tsp ground cumin
2 tsp paprika
1 tsp ground coriander
finely grated zest of ½ orange (see Top Tip, page 93)

✅ Top Tips
- You could use any canned pulses in this curry, such as butter beans, black-eyed peas or brown lentils.
- You can use 1 vegetable stock cube dissolved in 250ml (9fl oz) boiling water.

Healthy and sustaining
Cheap eat
Comfort food
Share with friends

MEAT-FREE MEALS

Nutritional Information (Per Serving)
302 calories, 10g fat (of which 1g saturates), 46g carbohydrate, 0.5g salt
Vegetarian

Serves 4
Preparation time 20 minutes
Cooking time about 40 minutes

263

Saag Aloo

2–3 tbsp vegetable oil
1 onion, peeled and finely sliced
2 garlic cloves, peeled and finely
    chopped
1 tbsp black mustard seeds
2 tsp ground turmeric
900g (2lb) potatoes, peeled and cut
    into chunks
1 tsp salt
4 handfuls baby spinach leaves

 1 Heat the oil in a pan and fry the onion over a medium heat for 10 minutes until golden, taking care not to burn it.

2 Add the garlic, mustard seeds and turmeric and cook for 1 minute. Add the potatoes, salt and 150ml (¼ pint) water. Cover the pan, bring to the boil, then reduce the heat and cook gently for 35–40 minutes or until tender. Add the spinach and cook until the leaves just wilt. Serve immediately.

 Moneysaver Tip
Instead of baby spinach leaves, use shredded spinach.

Top Tip
To make the curry into a complete meal, add 400g can chickpeas or other beans, rinsed and drained, then cook for 5–10 minutes before adding the spinach.

Healthy choice
Cheap eat
Comfort food
Share with friends

Serves 4
Preparation time 15 minutes
Cooking time 55 minutes

Nutritional Information (Per Serving)
295 calories, 10g fat (of which 1g saturates), 47g carbohydrate, 0.2g salt
Vegetarian · Gluten free · Dairy free · Easy

Veggie Curry

1 Heat the curry paste in a large heavy-based pan for 1 minute, stirring the paste to warm the spices. Add the tomatoes and hot stock. Bring to the boil, then reduce the heat to a simmer and add the vegetables. Simmer for 5–6 minutes until the vegetables are tender.

2 Stir in the chickpeas and heat for 1–2 minutes until hot. Serve the vegetable curry with a griddled wholemeal pitta and yogurt.

1 tbsp medium curry paste
227g can chopped tomatoes
150ml (¼ pint) hot vegetable stock (see Top Tip)
200g (7oz) vegetables, such as broccoli, courgettes and sugarsnap peas, roughly chopped
½ × 400g can chickpeas, drained and rinsed

✓ Top Tip
You can use ½ stock cube dissolved in 150ml (¼ pint) boiling water.

Ready in under 30 minutes
Healthy and sustaining
Comfort food
Share with friends

MEAT-FREE MEALS

Nutritional Information (Per Serving)
299 calories, 10g fat (of which 1g saturates), 32g carbohydrate, 2.3g salt
Dairy free · Vegetarian · Easy

Serves 1
Preparation time 5 minutes
Cooking time 12 minutes

265

Sweet Things

Orange Eggy Bread

Sweet Kebabs

Strawberry and Chocolate Muffins

Cherry Yogurt Crush

Fruity Fool

Lemon and Passion Fruit Fool

Quick Lemon Mousse

Cheat's Chocolate Pots

Grilled Coconut Cake

Roasted Apples with Oats and Blueberries

Cinnamon Pancakes

Quick Chocolate Slices

Pear and Blackberry Crumble

Express Apple Tart

Panettone Pudding

Three Quick Sauces for Ice Cream

Orange Eggy Bread

2 large eggs
150ml (¼ pint) milk
finely grated zest of 1 orange
    (see Top Tip, page 93)
50g (2oz) butter
8 slices raisin bread, halved
    diagonally
1 tbsp caster sugar
vanilla ice cream and orange
    segments to serve

1 Lightly whisk the eggs, milk and orange zest together in a bowl.

2 Heat the butter in a large frying pan over a medium heat. Dip the slices of raisin bread into the egg mixture and fry on both sides until golden.

3 Sprinkle the bread with the sugar and serve immediately with ice cream and orange slices.

Ready in under 30 minutes
Quick and easy
Cheap eat
Comfort food

Serves 4
Preparation time 10 minutes
Cooking time 15 minutes

Nutritional Information (Per Serving)
358 calories, 13g fat (of which 7g saturates), 54g carbohydrate, 1.2g salt
Vegetarian · Easy

Sweet Kebabs

1 Preheat the grill or barbecue. Spear alternate chunks of chocolate brownie and strawberries on to skewers. Grill or barbecue for 3 minutes, turning occasionally. Serve with whipped cream.

chocolate brownie, about 10 x 5cm (4 x 2in), cut into eight chunks
8 large strawberries
whipped cream to serve

Ready in under 30 minutes
Quick and easy
Five ingredients or fewer
Cheap eats

Nutritional Information (Per Serving)
521 calories, 23g fat (of which 12g saturates), 77g carbohydrate, 0.3g salt
Vegetarian • Easy

Serves 4
Preparation time 5 minutes
Cooking time 3 minutes

Strawberry and Chocolate
Muffins

2 chocolate muffins, halved
4 tbsp mascarpone or cream cheese,
    softened
600g (1lb 5oz) strawberries, hulled
    and roughly chopped
plain chocolate, grated, to decorate

 Divide the muffin halves among four plates. Top each half with a tablespoon of the cheese and a good spoonful of strawberries.

2 Sprinkle with the grated chocolate and serve immediately.

Ready in under 30 minutes
Quick and easy
Five ingredients or fewer
Comfort food

270

Serves 4
Preparation time 5 minutes

Nutritional Information (Per Serving)
420 calories, 20g fat (of which 12g saturates), 55g carbohydrate, 0.6g salt
Vegetarian · Easy

Cherry Yogurt Crush

1 Spoon some cherries into the bottom of each of four 400ml (14fl oz) glasses. Top with a dollop of yogurt and some biscuits. Continue layering up each glass until all the ingredients have been used.

2 Chill for 15 minutes–2 hours before serving.

400g can stoned cherries, drained, or 450g (1lb) fresh cherries, stoned
500g (1lb 2oz) Greek yogurt
150g (5oz) macaroons

£ **Moneysaver Tip**
Instead of macaroons use broken HobNobs or shortbread biscuits.

Quick and easy
Five ingredients or fewer
Comfort food
Share with friends

SWEET THINGS

Nutritional Information (Per Serving)
390 calories, 18g fat (of which 9g saturates), 45g carbohydrate, 0.5g salt
Vegetarian

Serves 4
Preparation time 10 minutes, plus chilling

Fruity Fool

500g carton summer fruit compôte
500g carton fresh custard

1 Divide half the compôte among six glasses, then add a thin layer of custard. Repeat the process until all the compôte and custard have been used.

2 Stir each fool once to swirl the custard and compôte together, then serve.

Ready in under 30 minutes
Quick and easy
Five ingredients or fewer
Cheap eat

Serves 6
Preparation time 2 minutes

Nutritional Information (Per Serving)
159 calories, 2g fat (of which trace saturates), 31g carbohydrate, 0.1g salt
Vegetarian · Gluten free · Easy

Lemon and Passion Fruit Fool

1 Put the lemon curd into a small bowl. Halve the passion fruits and spoon the pulp into a sieve resting over a bowl. Stir to separate the seeds from the juice. Add 1 tbsp of the passion fruit juice to the lemon curd and mix well.

2 In a large bowl, whip the cream with the icing sugar until soft peaks form. Stir in the yogurt.

3 Put a dollop of yogurt cream into each of six small glasses. Layer with a spoonful of lemon curd mixture and 1 tsp passion fruit juice. Repeat to use up all the ingredients. Scatter some toasted flaked almonds on top and serve immediately.

6 tbsp lemon curd
4 ripe passion fruits
150ml (¼ pint) double cream
1 tbsp icing sugar
200g (7oz) Greek yogurt
toasted flaked almonds to decorate

Ready in under 30 minutes
Quick and easy
Comfort food
Share with friends

SWEET THINGS

Nutritional Information (Per Serving)
210 calories, 17g fat (of which 10g saturates), 14g carbohydrate, 0.1g salt
Vegetarian · Gluten free · Easy

Serves 6
Preparation time 20 minutes

Quick Lemon Mousse

6 tbsp lemon curd
300ml (½ pint) double cream,
  whipped
fresh berries to decorate

1 Gently stir the lemon curd through the double cream until combined and decorate with berries.

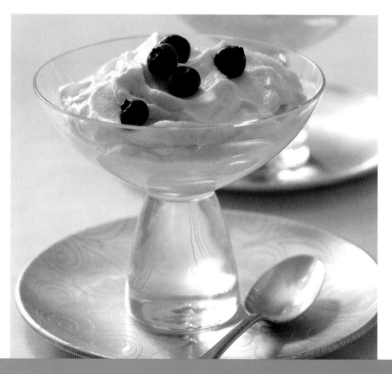

Ready in under 30 minutes
Quick and easy
Five ingredients or fewer
Cheap eat

Serves 4
Preparation time 1–2 minutes

Nutritional Information (Per Serving)
334 calories, 30g fat (of which 18g saturates), 16g carbohydrate, 0.1g salt
Vegetarian · Gluten free · Easy

Cheat's Chocolate Pots

 Put the custard into a small pan with the chocolate pieces. Heat gently, stirring all the time, until the chocolate has melted.

2 Pour the mixture into four small cups or glasses and chill in the fridge for 30 minutes to 1 hour before serving.

500g carton fresh custard
200g (7oz) plain chocolate, broken
     into pieces

Try Something Different
Serve the mixture warm as a sauce for vanilla ice cream.

Quick and easy
Five ingredients or fewer
Cheap eat
Comfort food

SWEET THINGS

Nutritional Information (Per Serving)
385 calories, 17g fat (of which 9g saturates), 53g carbohydrate, 0.1g salt
Vegetarian · Easy

Serves 4
Preparation time 5 minutes, plus chilling
Cooking time 5 minutes

275

Grilled Coconut Cake

4 thick slices coconut or Madeira cake
icing sugar to dust
Greek yogurt or crème fraîche and
　　fresh fruit to serve

1 Preheat the grill. Grill the cake until lightly charred on both sides. Dust with icing sugar and serve with thick Greek yogurt and fresh fruit, cut into bite-size pieces.

Ready in under 30 minutes
Quick and easy
Cheap eat
Comfort food

Serves 4
Preparation time 5 minutes
Cooking time 5 minutes

Nutritional Information (Per Serving)
434 calories, 24g fat (of which 0g saturates), 51g carbohydrate, 1g salt
Vegetarian · Easy

Roasted Apples with Oats
and Blueberries

1 Preheat the oven to 200°C (180°C fan oven) mark 6. Core the apples, then use a sharp knife to score around the middle of each (this will stop the apple from collapsing). Put the apples into a roasting tin.

2 Put the pecan nuts into a bowl together with the oats, blueberries and sugar. Mix together, then spoon into the apples, pour 1 tbsp orange juice over each apple and bake in the oven for 30–40 minutes until the apples are soft.

4 cooking apples (see Top Tip)
25g (1oz) pecan nuts, chopped
25g (1oz) rolled (porridge) oats
50g (2oz) blueberries
2 tbsp light muscovado sugar
4 tbsp orange juice

 Top Tip
Apples are easy to work with because they are very firm-fleshed, but their flesh turns brown when exposed to air and starts to discolour quickly. Toss with lemon juice if you are not going to use the prepared fruit immediately.

**Comfort food
Share with friends**

SWEET THINGS

Nutritional Information (Per Serving)
164 calories, 5g fat (of which trace saturates), 29g carbohydrate, 0g salt
Vegetarian · Dairy free · Easy

Serves 4
Preparation time 15 minutes
Cooking time 30–40 minutes

Cinnamon Pancakes

150g (5oz) plain flour
½ tsp ground cinnamon
1 medium egg
300ml (½ pint) skimmed milk
olive oil to fry
fruit compôte or sugar and Greek
    yogurt to serve

1 Put the flour, cinnamon, egg and milk into a large bowl and whisk together to make a smooth batter. Leave to stand for 20 minutes.

2 Heat a heavy-based frying pan over a medium heat. When the pan is really hot, add 1 tsp oil, pour in a ladleful of batter and tilt the pan to coat the bottom of the pan with an even layer of batter. Cook for 1 minute or until golden. Flip the pancake over and cook for 1 minute. Remove the pancake from the pan and put on to a warmed plate. Repeat with the remaining batter, adding more oil if necessary, to make six pancakes. Serve with a fruit compôte or a sprinkling of sugar, and a dollop of yogurt.

Try Something Different

- Sprinkle the cooked pancakes with caster sugar and squeeze lemon juice over.
- Spread the pancakes with 1 tbsp chocolate spread and top with sliced banana.
- Serve with sliced bananas and vanilla ice cream instead of the fruit compôte and yogurt.

Ready in under 30 minutes
Quick and easy
Cheap eat
Comfort food

Serves 6
Preparation time 5 minutes
Cooking time 20 minutes

Nutritional Information (Per Serving)
141 calories, 5g fat (of which 1g saturates), 20g carbohydrate, 0.1g salt
Vegetarian · Easy

Quick Chocolate Slices

1 Put the butter or olive oil spread in a heatproof bowl and add the golden syrup and cocoa. Melt in a 900W microwave on full power for 20 seconds or until melted, or melt in a pan over a very low heat. Mix everything together.

2 Remove from the heat and stir in the biscuits. Mix well until thoroughly coated in chocolate, crushing down any large pieces of biscuit.

3 Turn into a greased 25.5 x 16.5cm (10 x 6½in) rectangular tin. Cool, cover and chill for 20 minutes.

4 Melt the chocolate in a heatproof bowl in a 900W microwave on full power for 1 minute 40 seconds, stirring twice. Or, put the bowl over a pan of gently simmering water, making sure the base of the bowl doesn't touch the water, and leave until melted. Stir once more and pour over the chocolate biscuit base, then chill for 20 minutes. Cut in half lengthways and cut each half into 20 rectangular fingers.

225g (8oz) butter or olive oil spread
3 tbsp golden syrup
50g (2oz) cocoa, sifted
300g pack digestive biscuits, crushed
400g (14oz) plain chocolate, broken
   into pieces

Five ingredients or fewer
Comfort food
Share with friends
Great for parties

Nutritional Information (Per Serving)
137 calories, 9g fat (of which 6g saturates), 13g carbohydrate, 0.3g salt
Vegetarian · Easy

Makes 40
Preparation time 10 minutes, plus
   chilling
Cooking time 2 minutes

Pear and Blackberry Crumble

450g (1lb) pears, peeled, cored and chopped, tossed with the juice of 1 lemon (see Top Tip, page 277)
225g (8oz) golden caster sugar
1 tsp mixed spice
450g (1lb) blackberries
cream, custard or ice cream to serve

FOR THE CRUMBLE TOPPING
100g (3½oz) butter, chopped, plus extra to grease
225g (8oz) plain flour
75g (3oz) ground almonds

1 Put the pears and lemon juice into a bowl, add 100g (3½oz) sugar and the mixed spice, then add the blackberries and toss thoroughly to coat.

2 Preheat the oven to 200°C (180°C fan oven) mark 6. Lightly butter a 1.8 litre (3¼ pint) shallow ovenproof dish, then carefully tip the fruit into the dish in an even layer.

3 To make the crumble topping, rub the butter into the flour in a large bowl by hand. Stir in the ground almonds and the remaining sugar. Bring parts of the mixture together with your hands to make lumps.

4 Spoon the crumble topping evenly over the fruit, then put into the oven and bake for 35–45 minutes until the fruit is tender and the crumble is golden and bubbling. Serve with cream, custard or ice cream.

✔ Top Tip
Crumble is a great way to use leftover, slightly overripe fruit. Replace the pears with apples, or omit the blackberries and use 700g (1½lb) plums or rhubarb instead. You could also use gooseberries (omit the spice), or try 450g (1lb) rhubarb with 450g (1lb) strawberries.

Comfort food
Share with friends

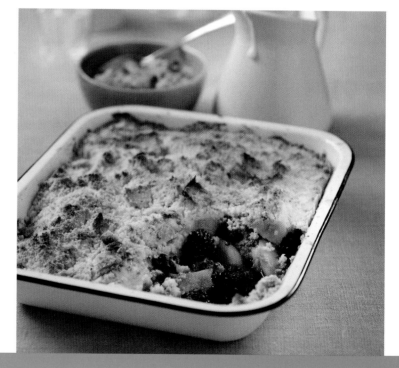

Serves 6
Preparation time 20 minutes
Cooking time 35–45 minutes

Nutritional Information (Per Serving)
525 calories, 21g fat (of which 9g saturates), 81g carbohydrate, 0.3g salt
Vegetarian • Easy

Express Apple Tart

1 Preheat the oven to 200°C (180°C fan oven) mark 6. Put the pastry on a 28 x 38cm (11 x 15in) baking sheet and lightly roll over it with a rolling pin to smooth down the pastry. Score lightly around the edge, leaving a 3cm (1¼ in) border.

2 Put the apple slices on top of the pastry within the border. Turn the edge of the pastry halfway over to reach the edge of the apples, press down and use your fingers to crimp the edge.

3 Dust heavily with icing sugar. Bake for 20 minutes or until the pastry is cooked and the sugar has caramelised. Serve warm, dusted with more icing sugar.

375g pack ready-rolled puff pastry
500g (1lb 2oz) dessert apples, such as Cox's, cored and thinly sliced, then tossed in the juice of 1 lemon (see Top Tip, page 277)
golden icing sugar to dust

Five ingredients or fewer
Cheap eat
Comfort food
Share with friends

SWEET THINGS

Nutritional Information (Per Serving)
197 calories, 12g fat (of which 0g saturates), 23g carbohydrate, 0.4g salt
Vegetarian · Easy

Serves 8
Preparation time 10 minutes
Cooking time 20 minutes

281

Panettone Pudding

400g (14oz) panettone, cut into 1cm
  (½ in) slices, then diagonally in
  half again to make triangles (see
  Moneysaver Tip)
4 medium eggs
450ml (¾ pint) milk
3 tbsp golden icing sugar

1 Preheat the oven to 180°C (160°C fan oven) mark 4. Arrange the slices of panettone in four 300ml (½ pint) gratin dishes or one 1.1 litre (1¾ pint) dish.

2 Beat the eggs, milk and 2 tbsp of the sugar in a bowl and pour over the panettone. Soak for 10 minutes.

3 Put the puddings or pudding in the oven and bake for 30–40 minutes. Dust with the remaining icing sugar to serve.

 Moneysaver Tip
Instead of panettone, use bread that
is very lightly buttered.

Five ingredients or fewer
Comfort food
Share with friends

Serves 4
Preparation time 10 minutes, plus
  10 minutes soaking
Cooking time 30–40 minutes

Nutritional Information (Per Serving)
450 calories, 13g fat (of which 5g saturates), 70g carbohydrate, 1.1g salt
Vegetarian • Easy

Three Quick Sauces
for Ice Cream

The Best Chocolate Sauce

Put 75g (3oz) roughly chopped plain chocolate into a small heatproof bowl set over a pan of simmering water, making sure the base of the bowl doesn't touch the water. Pour in 150ml (¼ pint) double cream, then leave the chocolate to melt over very low heat. It will take about 10 minutes. Don't stir, or it will thicken to a sticky mess. Once melted, gently stir until smooth. Serve with ice cream or poached pears.

Try Something Different

- Add a shot of espresso coffee to the cream and chocolate while they're melting together.
- Use mint-flavoured chocolate instead of plain.

Butterscotch Sauce

Heat 50g (2oz) butter, 50g (2oz) golden caster sugar, 75g (3oz) light muscovado sugar and 150g (5oz) golden syrup together gently, stirring, until melted. Cook for 5 minutes, then remove from the heat. Stir in 125ml (4fl oz) double cream, a few drops of vanilla extract and the juice of ½ lemon and stir over a low heat for 1–2 minutes.

Strawberry Sauce

Put 225g (8oz) hulled strawberries and 2–3 tbsp icing sugar in blender and whiz well to combine. Alternatively, mash well with a fork or potato masher. Sieve the sauce and chill until needed.

Ready in under 30 minutes
Quick and easy
Comfort food
Share with friends

SWEET THINGS

Index